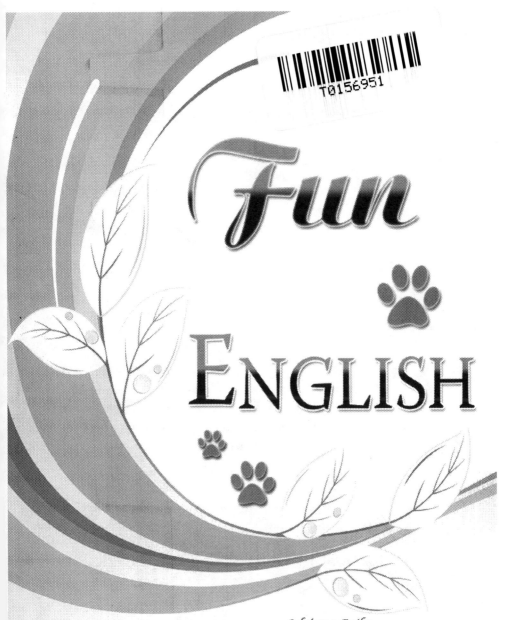

Fun

ENGLISH

Adriana Bejko

Book 4
Sound it out!

To order additional copies of this book, contact:
Xlibris Corporation
1-888-795-4274
www.Xlibris.com
Orders@Xlibris.com
92193

CONTENTS

READING	WRITING	VOCABULARY DEVELOPMENT	LANGUAGE STRUCTURE	REVIEW
LESSON 1 English Alphabet	punctuations, capital letters, full stops; Liking Ideas— using "and" & "but" to join sentences Rules— learning English letters and sounds	letter(s), the, say, sound(s), alphabet, know, name(s), remember, hard, question(s), hard different, right, problem(s), tool(s), spelling, properly, to check, correct, everyone, certain, exist, recognize, (to) sound, spell, mark, something, by heart, don't worry, proof reading, right, mistake(s), place, rules of pronunciation, I am ready, champion, importance of learning, test your knowledge, mean, province, explain, express, agreement, idea(s), (to) hand, important, depend, want, think, look, the same, need, true, understand, a lot		day(s), class(es), student(s),come, learn, some, but, new, words, this things, read, sit, teacher(s), help classroom(s). computer(s), sentence(s), sometimes, strong because, tomorrow
LESSON 2 Beginning Consonants		consonant(s), we, beginning, too, yesterday, clear, afternoon, went-go, vocabulary, are		word(s), new, learn, day(s), help, say, spring, different, nice,

		speaking, voice(s), paper(s), collect, improve, easy, exercise(s), enjoyed, vowel(s), there are, practice, express, I am so proud of you, it is my pleasure, I am able, make mistakes, all of you, pay attention to . . . . , practice makes perfect		warm, many, flower(s), spell, learned, was hard, to hand in, problem(s), question(s)
LESSON 3 Short Vowels "a", "o", and "æ"		I am so sorry, no worries, it is fine, have a sore throat, I am sure, take good notes, are/am/ going to . . . . late, told/ tell, come, concerned, what, sick, think, play(ed), ice, why, water, throat(s), how, can, phone, give, idea(s), hope, wonderful, the same, apple(s), us, hope, international, system(s), correct, symbol(s), must, pronounce, even, pronunciation, let us		it is, nice, yellow, student(s), today, classroom(s), school(s), speak, improve, voice(s), yesterday, went, afternoon, clear, home(s), paper(s), because, cherries, flower(s), too, strawberries, ask, agree, exercise(s), collect, practice, everybody, need, question(s), mean, excited, expression(s), sound(s)

LESSON		Some, province(s), territory, yesterday, question(s), focus, that, understand, same, research, do, problem (s), decision(s), federal, government(s), area(s), largest, fat, newspaper, part(s), divide(d), call(ed), equal. capital(s), population, above dogsled(s), to fish, snowmobile(s), to hunt, seal(s), meat boot(s), skin, right, help(ed), which, think/thought, change(d), their, month(s), frozen, vocabulary, made, find/found, up, magazine(s), move different, used, improve(d), of course, I am not sure, in the old days, on the other hand, airplane(s), move around, food(s), lamp oil, difference, between, constitutional, power(s), govern		come, they, want, learn, new, today, lesson, country, classroom, go, anybody, thank you, answer(s), spring, winter, what, animal, people
4—My New Country & Ending Sounds				

LESSON 5		discussion(s), to		province, start,
Facts About		present, collect, to		territory, focus,
Canada & **"th"**		show, important,		research, their,
Sound		library, easy, glad,		question(s),
		drawing(s), choose,		today,
		idea(s), smart, way,		homework,
		although, inhabit,		everyone, was
		interesting, skill(s),		sure, found,
		walrus, feed, of		area, some,
		course, protect, sea,		different,
		prepare, something,		animals(s), is
		listen, leave, all kinds		made up of,
		of, take care of, at		want warm,
		first, deep, cry, are		survival,
		born, also, month(s),		of course,
		cub(s)		anybody,
LESSON 6		immigrant(s),		learn, sound(s),
Words from		main, topic(s),		both, glad,
Immigrants		bring(brought),		some, know.
& Confusing		contribution(s),		word(s),
Letters		special, confusing,		language(s),
		good(better), ham,		different, focus,
		employment,		discussion(s),
		become, enrich,		of course,
		responsibility,		important,
		sometimes, easy,		problems,
		example(s), true,		leave,
		history, easy, think,		population,
		connected, share,		ways part(s),
		seaport(s), food,		town(s), right,
		European(s), patty,		travel
		bun(s), line(s),		
		ate(eat), grill, serve		
		understand, getting		
		older, on the other		
		hand, make/ made		
		out of, appoint, to		
		form, exist, in fact,		

		at that time, ground beef, popular, fast, which, confuse, pronounce		
CHECK YOUR KNOWLEDGE —Progress Test				
LESSON 7 Animal World & Short and Long Vowel "u"		insect(s), science, weather, go-went, shelter(s), pet, until, adopt, milk, drink, goat(s), always, dirty, mud, must, never, lamb(s), breakfast, sometimes, hen(s) duck(s), pick out, fresh food, trip, rooster(s), take a break, camping, share, duckling(s), year(s), family, bee(s), butterfly, ladybug(s), worm(s), honey, antenna(s), male, wing(s), pretty, woods, bite, ruin, mosquito(s), female(s), protein produce, feed on, prevent, perfume		discussion, focus, animals, cow, too, interesting, smart, understand, like, special, which, form, anybody, little, summer, think, anything, know, read, right, because, exercise, warm, a lot of, beautiful, grass, eat, field, class, word, play, about, discuss, story, confused, smell, something
LESSON 8 Celebrations & Short Vowel "i"		holiday(s), scary, celebration(s), celebrate, glorious, notice, marvelous, October, television, typical, ghost(s)		question, fall, main, days, trees, seasons, special, beautiful, right, eye, people,

		neighbourhood, character(s), silly, poor, experience, promise(s), the dead, pray, treat(s), candy, thankful, decorate, need, ornament(s), under, tie, bow, come, present(s), ready, stocking(s), All Souls Day, trick-and-treat, drop out, in front of, popular, lovely, jack-o-lantern, make sure, wake up, turned, delicious		blood, talk about, sound, think, go/went, house, popular, children, library, help, a lot of, connect, the same, different, sometimes, share, wavy lines, some, painted, lemon cake, about
LESSON 9 Travelling & Short Vowel **"e"**		travelling, trip(s), difficult, driving, storm(s), road(s), slippery, usually, bus, train(s), drive-drop, ride, plane(s), appointment(s), bicycle(s), nervous, during, vacation(s), place(s), last, visit, ferry, take/took, faster, truck(s), passing, conductor, homophones(s), synonym(s), have the chance, I am sorry, antonym(s), come across, make a point, explain, meaning(s), alike, spelling,		student, come, old, country, leave-left, share, experiences, must, morning, winter, night, car, cold, night, go, summer, live, too, different, house, grandmother, something, important

		another, almost, need, opposite, practice, concept(s), agree, totally, exercise(s	
LESSON 10 My Body, My Health & Short **"a+r"**		proficiency, especially, pronunciation, spelling, communicate, connect, health, medicine, toes, cardiologist, accident(s), itchy, become, patient(s), peely, blister(s), sign(s), treated, cracked, skin, important, scratch, spread, share, bad, smoking, habit(s), drug(s), mind, decision(s), tobacco, contain, substance(s), addictive, cigarette(s) cigar(s), work hard, right now, grow up, pay attention, no matter, poison(s), peer pressure, make healthy choices, heart(s), mouth(s), attack, all at once, keep in mind, throat(s), lung(s), pollute, breath, affect, appearance(s), exposure(s), accept, world, fingernail(s),		happy, students, know, word, trip, expressions, road. today, body, dry, slippery, come, home, usually, doctor, situation, sounds, difficult, easily, show, drawing, something, smell, called, remember

		million(s),unique, magazine(s), age, fabulous, inside, attractive, brace(s)		
LESSON 11 Emotional Health & Hard and Soft "**c**"		believe, feeling(s), continue, same, topic(s), behavior, stress, happen, relationship(s), disrupt, sadness, anxiety, main, characteristic(s), deal with, death, move to, change(s), stressful, affect, respond, upset, connection(s), disease(s), develop, pain(s), appetite, headache, gain, emotional health, be aware of, cope with stress, be interested in . . . , lose the job, lose weight, lose, get married, weight, get divorced, high blood pressure, keep in mind, make time for . . . , exercising, alcohol, recognize, cause(s), inside, outside, bothering, social, counselor(s), balanced, calm, journal(s), sleep, resilience, support, accept, relaxation, meditation, regular		discussions, healthy, choices, yesterday, today, think, important, comments, sick, child, situation, medicine, sound, especially, strong, tobacco, drug, take, take care, find, share, focus, someone, happy, improve, number, research

| LESSON 12 Shopping for Clothes & Hard and Soft "g" | | interested, hate. department store, develop, exactly, situation(s), dress shoes, participate, related, lace(s), too big, wear, size(s), half, try on, right(a), right(b), helpful, to check, the cheque, dictionary, go shopping, window shop, vocabulary, driver`s license, are going to . . . . , peers, list(s), expand, excuse me, over there, how about . . . . , need, how much, on sale, go ahead, in order to, fitting room, maxed out, make proud, towel(s), buckle(s), high heel(s), add, rack, sportswear, fit aisle(s), sweater(s), politely, hanger, almost, tax, comes to . . . . , I.D. or ID, compiler, clerk(s), discount, price(s), explanation(s), bar, item(s), spending, interesting, reach, limit(s) | | ornaments, totally, enjoy, stressful, agree, disrupted, today, usually, different, relationships, kind, main, character, share, words, improve, experiences, proficiency |
| PROGRESS EXAM | | | | |

Assignments Record

#	Assignment Page #	Lesson	Date Completed	Got it! Mark	Still unclear
1					
2					
3					
4					
5					
6					
7	Exam				
8					
9					
10					
11					
12					
13					
14	Progress Test				

Introductions: Our story happens in a school where students learn English as a foreign (EFL) or as an additional language (EAL). There are many students who learn English in this school and they have many teachers—Mr. Knowitall, Dr. Alba, Miss Lovely, etc. We have already been introduced to Miss Lovely through our first three books. Let us go now to Mr. Knowitall's class and get to know the teacher and his students. Here they are:

Lesson 1—English Alphabet

Learning goals: A. Learn the alphabet
B. Learn how to write the letters
C. Learn how to say the words

(**The Author:** It is the first day of classes. Students in Mr. Knowitall's class come from many countries of the world to learn English in Canada. Students know some words in English but they will learn more about letters, sounds, spelling, and reading in this class. To achieve this goal they need to first learn the letters of the English alphabet. Students are sitting in the classroom waiting for Mr. Knowitall, their Canadian teacher.)

Mr. Knowitall: (enters the classroom and greets his students) Good morning everyone. Welcome to our English class where we will learn about English **sounds**, **letters** and words. Does **anybody know** the English **alphabet**? Please, **say** your **name** when you answer because we want to get to know each other.

Ben: (wants to stand up before answering, as he did in his home country, but **remembers** that in Canada students do not stand up to answer the teacher's **question**. So, he sits down.) My name is Ben and I am from India. I know the English alphabet. (says the alphabet: a b c d e f g . . . .)

Stephen: (speaks with a strong voice) Good morning everyone! I am Stephen and I come from Sudan. I know how to say the alphabet **by heart** but it is **hard** for me to write the letters because in my first language we write with **different** letters. So, I have **problems** with the **spelling** of the words.

Paolo: (**excited** that he knows how to use the computer **to check** the spelling) Hi guys, I am Paolo and I have just **arrived** from the

Philippines. Stephen, **don't worry** about spelling, my friend. There is a **spelling check tool** in the computer.

Mr. Knowitall: Welcome to our class, Paolo. Yes, you are **correct**, but there are two problems with the computer spelling check: 1) not **everyone** knows how to use a computer, and 2) in English there are some words that **sound** the same but we spell them differently. So, sometimes the spelling check does not help because the spelling of a **certain** word may **exist** and the computer **recognizes** the word but that is not the **right** word for your sentence.

Karol: (**shy** and **embarrassed** to speak) Hi, my name is Karol and I come from Colombia. I have learned the English alphabet and it is not very different from my first language. Knowing the alphabet helps us learn good spelling. Our English teacher in Colombia taught us about **something** called **"proof reading"**. That helps us correct the spelling **mistakes** before we give the home-work to the teacher **to mark**.

Ming: (speaks with a **strong voice**) Hi, my name is Ming and I come from China. I am the **champion** of Kong Fu for my **province**, Sichuan. I do not know the English alphabet and it is very different from my first language, Chinese. Mr. Knowitall, I also do not know what "proof reading" **means**. Can you **explain** that to us, please? (some students **express agreement** and say: "Yes, please.")

Mr. Knowitall: I would be happy to explain this **idea.** Proofreading is very **important**. When we do proofreading we check the writing and correct any mistakes before we **hand** the home-work to the teacher. At the beginning, some of us may not see the mistakes, such as wrong spelling, because we may not recognize which words are not correct. So, it is very important to read your home-work again and correct any mistakes. Yes, there is a spelling check in the computer but good students do not **depend** on the computer only for the spell check. Doing a good proofreading of writing is very important.

Monique: Hi, I am Monique and I come from Congo. I am so excited to learn English. Thank you Mr. Knowitall, now I know what proofreading is and I will use it in the future.

Ming: (**agrees** with Monique) Thank you Mr. Knowitall. I am very happy to learn English and speak to my new Canadian and international friends.

Mr. Knowitall: If that is what you **want** Ming, you are in the **right place** to learn English in our school. (turns to other students) Do you know how many letters are there in the English alphabet?

George: Hi, I am George and I come from Sweden. I **think** there are twenty six (26) letters in the English alphabet.

Ben: I agree with George. I think there are twenty six letters, too. I also think that learning how to use the English alphabet is very important for learning **new** words.

Karol: Spanish alphabet <u>looks</u> the same as the English alphabet but the <u>**rules of pronunciation**</u> and writing in English are very different from the rules of Spanish. I know that and I need to learn those rules.

George: Swedish uses <u>**the same**</u> alphabet as English, too, but I agree with Karol, we <u>**need**</u> to learn the rules of pronunciation in English.

Monique: That is <u>**true**</u> for French, my first language, too. So, I <u>**am ready**</u> and excited to learn English pronunciation rules. There are pronunciation rules in English, Mr. Knowitall, aren't there?

Mr. Knowitall: I am happy that all of you <u>**understand**</u> the <u>**importance of learning**</u> the rules of <u>**using**</u> the English alphabet to learn more new words. This is very important.

Paolo: Can we use the computer to learn more words, Mr. Knowitall?

Stephen: (laughs) Come on, Paolo. Computers are not <u>**everything**</u>.

Mr. Knowitall: In fact, computers may **help** us **a lot** if we use them **properly**. For example, for **tomorrow**, you can **test your knowledge** of the alphabet by doing the exercises on the following website: http://www.learnenglish.org.uk/kids/antics/index.html[1]. That is your home-work; it will be so much fun doing the homework on your computers. See you tomorrow everybody and thank you for a great class today.

Practice Your Knowledge

Exercise #1—Vocabulary study

Task 1—Check the meaning of the following words in your dictionary. Copy the definitions: e. x. **"sound"**—something that we hear. I like the sounds of birds on the trees in spring.

Task 2—Find the sentence with the same word from the text and copy it or write your own sentence. Follow the example with the first word "sound": **sound(s)**

Definition—something that can be heard
Sentence—I listen to the sounds of birds singing on the trees.

❑ **letter(s)**
Definition ....
Sentence ....

[1] © British Council. The British Council is the United Kingdom's international organization for educational and cultural relations.

- ❑ **anybody**

Definition ....

Sentence ....

- ❑ **know**

Definition ....

Sentence ....

- ❑ **alphabet**

Definition ....

Sentence ....

- ❑ **say**

Definition ....

Sentence ....

- ❑ **name**

Definition ....

Sentence ....

- ❑ **remember**

Definition ....

Sentence ....

- ❑ **question(s)**

Definition ....

Sentence ....

- ❑ **hard**

Definition ....

Sentence ....

- ❑ **different**

Definition ....

Sentence ....

- ❑ **problem(s)**

Definition ....

Sentence ....

- ❑ **spelling**

Definition ....

Sentence ....

- ❑ **excited**

Definition ....

Sentence ....

- ❑ **to check**

Definition ....

Sentence ....

❑ **arrive**

Definition ....

Sentence ....

❑ **tool(s)**

Definition ....

Sentence ....

❑ **correct**

Definition ....

Sentence ....

❑ **everyone**

Definition ....

Sentence ....

❑ **certain**

Definition ....

Sentence ....

❑ **exist**

Definition ....

Sentence ....

❑ **recognize**

Definition ....

Sentence ....

❑ **right/correct**

Definition ....

Sentence ....

❑ **shy**

Definition ....

Sentence ....

❑ **embarrassed**

Definition ....

Sentence ....

❑ **something**

Definition ....

Sentence ....

❑ **mistake(s)**

Definition ....

Sentence ....

❑ **mark**

Definition ....

Sentence ....

❑ **voice**

Definition ....

Sentence ....

❑ **champion(s)**

Definition ....

Sentence ....

❑ **province(s)**

Definition ....

Sentence ....

❑ **idea(s)**

Definition ....

Sentence ....

❑ **to hand**

Definition ....

Sentence ....

❑ **important**

Definition ....

Sentence ....

❑ **depend**

Definition ....

Sentence ....

❑ **agree**

Definition ....

Sentence ....

❑ **think**

Definition ....

Sentence ....

❑ **new**

Definition ....

Sentence ....

❑ **look**

Definition ....

Sentence ....

❑ **same**

Definition ....

Sentence ....

❑ **understand**

Definition ....

Sentence ....

❑ **use**
Definition ....
Sentence..

❑ **everything**
Definition ....
Sentence..

❑ **help**
Definition ....
Sentence..

❑ **a lot**
Definition ....
Sentence..

❑ **properly**
Definition ....
Sentence..

❑ **tomorrow**
Definition ....
Sentence..

write on!

Exercise # 2-Write the alphabet letters that are missing, use the proper order.

___	b	___	d	___			
___	___	h	___	___			
k	___	___	___	o	___	___	r
___	t	___	v	___	x	___	z

(Check this website to help you with reviewing the alphabet:

http://www.ngfl-cymru.org.uk/vtc/ngfl/ngfl-flash/alphabet-eng/alphabet.htm)

Exercise # 3—Say the name of the object in the picture.

Write the beginning sound under the picture, e. x.
say: "fish" and write "**f**" under the picture.

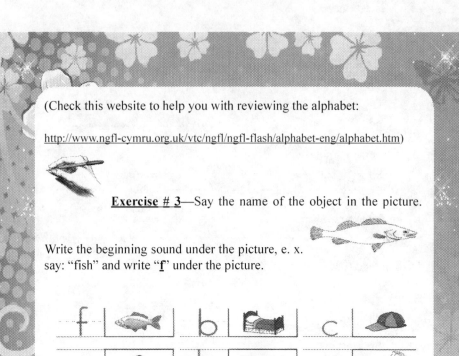

Exercise # 4—Work with a friend. Discover the secret picture. Draw a line from letter A to letter Z following the correct alphabet order. Say the letters as you draw. Tell your friend what you discovered.

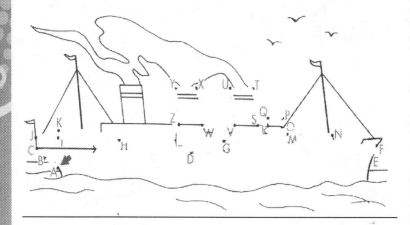

Exercise # 5—Find the secret word and write a sentence with it.

❖ snuods---

❖ tetelrs---

❖ obydayn---

- ❖ bememerr--
- ❖ eeeoyrvn--
- ❖ geoiercnz---
- ❖ ioattnrpm---
- ❖ ueannddstr--
- ❖ eeyignhtrv---
- ❖ ooowrrmt--

Home-work—Test your knowledge of the English alphabet. Do the exercises on the following website: http://www.learnenglish.org. uk/kids/antics/index.html

STUDY TIP-If you want to remember the words you learned, write, draw, and say each word five (5) times. Write a sentence with each new word.

....
....
....

SPOT THE MISTAKE-Find the mistakes and fix them. Write the correct sentence:

This dog   is brown...
....
....

REMEMBER THIS—Mr. John Cabot (Giovanni Cappotto) was the first explorer to come to Canada in 1497.

DID YOU KNOW?—Canadians consume more macaroni and cheese than any other nation in the world.

LANGUAGE BANK—In this lesson you learned:

Active words	Recycled words	Passive words
1. letter(s)	1. day(s)	1. country
2. the sound(s)	2. class(es)	2. world(s)
3. alphabet	3. student(s)	3. about
4. know	4. come	4. anybody
5. say	5. learn	5. achieve
6. name(s)	6. some	6. goal(s)
7. remember	7. word(s)	7. need
8. question(s)	8. but	8. wait
9. hard	9. new	9. enter
10. different	10. thing(s)	10. greet
11. problem(s)	11. read	11. shy
12. spelling	12. this	12. embarrassed
13. properly	13. sit	13. excited
14. to check	14. classroom(s)	14. voice(s)
15. tool(s)	15. teacher(s)	15. agree
16. correct	16. computer(s)	16. using
17. everyone	17. sentence(s)	17. everything
18. certain	18. sometimes	
19. exist	19. because	
20. recognize	20. help	
21. right	21. strong	
22. (to) sound	22. tomorrow	
23. spell		
24. mark		

25. something
26. mistake(s)
27. champion(s)
28. province
29. mean
30. explain
31. express
32. agreement(s)
33. idea(s)
34. (to) hand
35. important
36. depend
37. want
38. think
39. look
40. the same
41. need
42. true
43. understand
44. a lot

Expressions: by heart, don't worry, proof reading, right place, rules of pronunciation, I am ready, importance of learning, test your knowledge

Lesson 2—Beginning Consonants

Learning goals: A. Learn beginning consonants
B. Learn English sounds and spelling
C. Learn more new words

(Today is the second day of classes and Mr. Knowitall will help his students learn how to say English consonants at the **beginning** of different words. Everyone is happy and excited to learn new things.)

Mr. Knowitall: (enters the classroom and greets his students) Good morning. Today is a nice autumn day. It is warm and many flowers are still blooming. The weather is very nice these days. Yesterday I went for a walk by the river. What did you do **yesterday afternoon**, Ben?

Ben: (thinks) Let me think, oh, yes I remember. I **went** with my mother to the Farmers' Market yesterday. **We** bought some fresh carrots, grapes, and strawberries.

Stephen: (smiles) Ben, Mr. Knowitall wants to know what you did to study English **vocabulary** and alphabet.

Ben: I know, I know. Yesterday afternoon, I **learned** the English alphabet and did my homework. I am very excited because I did not make any mistakes.

Paolo: Mr. Knowitall, I learned the English alphabet yesterday afternoon, **too**. I liked using the computer and the website you gave to us. I know that the alphabet is very important and will help us to learn the new words and write better, too.

Mr. Knowitall: **I am so proud of** you both. You learned different letters and sounds yesterday and now **are speaking** with a **clear** and strong **voice** today.

Karol: It was hard for me to remember the alphabet but I learned how to write all the letters because I know it will help me write well. Can I hand in my **paper** with the home-work to you, Mr. Knowitall?

Mr. Knowitall: Yes, please. Carol. Can you **collect** your friends' papers, too?

Karol: **It is my pleasure.** (starts to collect everybody's papers).

Ming: Mr. Knowitall, at the beginning I had some problems with the alphabet, too, but now **I am able** to recognize all the letters of the English alphabet and connect them to the correct sounds and pronunciation.

Mr. Knowitall: Everyone **makes mistakes** at the beginning but now you recognize the English letters and sounds and remember how to use them properly. That is very important.

Monique: I think my spelling and writing will **improve** now because I know the alphabet. I am very excited to learn English and learn more about Canada.

Ming: At the beginning I was embarrassed to say the alphabet because I made so many mistakes but now I know the alphabet and I am very excited.

Mr. Knowitall: I agree with **all of you**. Did you do the **exercises** in the website I gave to you as a home-work?

George: Yes, I did the exercises and **enjoyed** that game, too. Learning in this class is very interesting and I had so much fun.

Ben: I did the exercises, too. They were not difficult, they were **easy**.

Karol: Mr. Knowitall, I can recognize the **consonants** and the **vowels** now and I can pronounce them properly.

George: I learned the consonants and the vowels, too, but I have a problem with the beginning consonants, Mr. Knowitall. How can I learn them better?

Mr. Knowitall: That is a very important question, George. Today we will learn how to **sound out** and how to spell the consonants at the beginning of the word. Please, **pay attention** to the exercises we will do. In English **there are** some rules but we need more **practice** to pronounce the sounds properly.

Monique: We learn more when we practice rules. I know an **expression** in English for this: "**Practice makes perfect.**"

Mr. Knowitall: That is a very good expression, Monique, and you are using it properly. Shall we start with our exercises now?

Practice Your Knowledge

write on!

Exercise #1—Vocabulary study.

Task 1—Check the meaning of the following words in your dictionary. Copy the definitions. e. x. **"sound"**—something that can be heard. In spring I hear the sounds of the birds on the trees.

Task 2—Find the sentence with the same word from the text and copy it or write your own sentence. Follow the example with the word "sound".

❑ **yesterday**
Definition ....
Sentence ....
❑ **afternoon**
Definition ....
Sentence ....
❑ **went / go**
Definition ....
Sentence ....

❑ **we**

Definition ....

Sentence ....

❑ **vocabulary**

Definition ....

Sentence ....

❑ **too**

Definition ....

Sentence ....

❑ **are speaking / speak**

Definition ....

Sentence ....

❑ **clear**

Definition ....

Sentence ....

❑ **paper**

Definition ....

Sentence ....

❑ **beginning**

Definition ....

Sentence ....

❑ **exercise(s)**

Definition ....

Sentence ....

❑ **enjoy / ed**

Definition ....

Sentence ....

❑ **they**

Definition ....

Sentence ....

❑ **easy**

Definition ....

Sentence ....

❑ **voice**

Definition ....

Sentence ....

❑ **collect**

Definition ....

Sentence ....

❑ **consonant(s)**
Definition ....
Sentence..
❑ **vowel(s)**
Definition ....
Sentence..
❑ **practice**
Definition ....
Sentence..
❑ **expression(s)**
Definition ....
Sentence..

Exercise #2—Find the word for the object, animal, or person in each picture. Circle the beginning sound.

p	d	s	c	t	s
m	ⓑ	k	x	h	f
t	c	d	s	p	r
q	b	t	c	b	q
f	w	d	q	t	r
u	x	c	s	f	e
b	p	l	r	m	k
q	i	q	g	i	n

write on!

Exercise # 3—Write the words below and say the first consonant, for example: Write: bird bird bird bird bird bird bird bird bird bird bird bird bird bird. Say: [b] bird

- dog _____
- pizza _____
- tree _____
- fish _____
- girl _____
- seal _____
- cat _____
- table _____
- monkey _____
- watermelon _____
- bear _____

Exercise #4—Directions: Say the alphabet letters aloud and find the missing letters in the following chart.

Check the alphabet here: **A-B-C-D-E-F-G-H-I-J-K-L-M-N-O-P-Q-R-S-T-U-V-W-X-Y-Z**

A B [ ] D E	F [ ] H I [ ]	K L [ ] N O
P [ ] S [ ] U	V [ ] X [ ] Z	

Repeat after me

Exercise # 5-Work with a friend. We must learn how to pronounce, read and write English words properly. If we learn the **INTERNATIONAL PHONETIC ALPHABET (IPA)** first, it is easy to learn how to pronounce the words properly. There are different IPA symbols that we need to learn to understand the pronunciation of the new words in the dictionary. Learn the IPA symbols from the following chart:

b	b	l	l	sh	ʃ	a	æ	oh ɔːʳ
p	p	r	ɹ	zh	ʒ	ah	aːʳ	oa o
d	d	m	m	th	θ	ay	e	u ʊ
t	t	n	n	h	h	e	ɛ	uh ʌ
f	f	s	s	w	w	ee	i	oo u
v	v	z	z	y	j	i	ɪ	oi ɔj
g	g	ch	tʃ	ng	ŋ	iy	aj	ow aw
k	k	j	dʒ			o	ɑ	

Exercise # 6—There are consonants and vowels in the English and they sound differently in different words. Let us learn them.

ENGLISH BEGINNING CONSONANTS:

B b [biː]

bear - [b ɛ ə]

bee - [biː]

bird - [b ə:d]

bat - [b æ t]

butterfly - ['b ʌ t ə flai]

beaver - ['biːv ə]

C c [siː]

cat - [k æ t]

cow - [kau]

chick - [tʃ ik]

camel - ['k æ m ə l]

crocodile - ['kr ɔ k ə dail]

chameleon - [k ə 'miːli ə n]

crayfish - ['kreifi ʃ]

crab - [kr æ b]

cake - [keik]

D d [diː]

donkey - ['d ɔ ŋ ki]

dog - [d ɔ g]

duck - [d ʌ k

deer - [diə]   **dove** - [dʌv]   **dolphin** - ['dɔlfin]

F f [ef]

fawn - [fɔn]   **fish** - [fiʃ]   **frog** - [frɔg]

fox - [fɔks]   **fly** - [flai]   **flamingo** - [flə'mingou]

G g [dʒiː]

giraffe - [dʒi'raːf]   **goose** - [guːs]   **goat** - [gout]

H h [eitʃ]

hen - [hen]   **hippopotamus** - [,hipə'pɔtəməs]   **horse** - [hɔːs]

J j ['dʒei]

jellyfish - ['dʒelifiʃ]

jackal - ['dʒækɔ:l]

jaguar - ['dʒægjuə]

K k [kei]

koala - [kou'a:lə]

kangaroo - [,kæŋgə'ru:]

kitten - ['kitn]

L l [el]

lion - ['laiən]

leopard - ['lepəd]

llama - ['la:mə]

lamb - [læm]

ladybird, ladybug - ['leidibəd or leidib ʌg]

M m [em]

mouse - [maus]

mice - [mais]

monkey - ['mʌnki]

mosquito –[m'ski:to]

N n [en]

nose - [nou'z]

newspaper - [nju:zpeipe]

P p [pi:]

pig - [pig]

piglet - ['piglit]

puppy - ['pʌpi]

parrot - ['pærət]

penguin - ['peŋgwin]

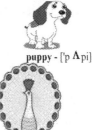

peacock - ['pi:kɔk]

Q q [kju:]

quail - [kweil]

question mark - ['kwestʃən ma:k]

R r [a:]

rhinoceros - [rai'nɔsərəs]

rabbit ['ræbit]

rooster ['ru:stə]

S s [es]

spider ['spaidə]

seal [si:l]

swan [swɔn]

sheep - [ʃi:p]

snail – [sneil]

snake – [sneik]

T t [ti:]

turtle - ['tɘ:tl]

turkey - ['tɘ:ki]

taxi -[tæksi]

V v [vi:]

vulture - ['vʌltʃɘ]

vine - [vain]

Valentine – [valɘntain]

W w [dʌblju:]

woodpecker - ['wudpekɘ]

whale - [weil]

wolf - [wulf]

X x [eks]

X-ray ['eksrei]

xerox machine – [zi:rɔks mɘʃi:n]

xylophone – [zai'lɔfɔn]

Y v [wai]

yak - [jæk]

yoyo – [jɔjɔ]

yarn – [ja:rn]

44

Z z [zed]

zebra - ['ziːbrə]

zipper – [ziːpə]

zoo – [zuː]

ENGLISH VOWELS

A a [ei]

animals - ['ænimls]

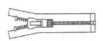

ant - [ænt]

alligator - ['æligeitə]

E e [iː]

eagle - ['iːgl]

eel - [iːl]

elephant - ['elifənt]

I i [ai]

iguana - [iˈgwaːnə]

insect - ['insekt]

O o [ou]

octopus - ['ktəpəs]

owl - [aul]

ostrich - ['ɔstritʃ]

otter - ['ɔtə]

ox - [ɔks]

U u [ju:]

unicorn - ['ju:nikɔ:n]

umbrella – [Λm'brelə]

Exercise #7-Find the secret word and write a sentence with it.

1. leovsw...
2. yyadesret...
3. nonoaretf...
4. yvroalcaub...
5. stconnnosa...

Exercise # 8-Practice the pronunciation of beginning sounds after discovering the secret words from Exercise #7.

Home-work—Use the English alphabet to discover and write the following sentence given to you in the International Phonetic Alphabet (IPA) [diə mʌðər, aɪ wɪl bi: leit tədeɪ]

STUDY TIP—When we study—**concentration is the key**—. Learning to concentrate while studying is a skill you will use for the rest of your life. The art of concentration is the ability to eliminate distractions and focus only on your task.

SPOT THE MISTAKE—The word for the boy in this picture

starts with a vowel and has four (4) consonants and three (3) vowels.

....
....
....

REMEMBER THIS—The English alphabet has 26 letters—twenty one (21) consonants and five (vowels).

DID YOU KNOW?—There is an International Phonetic Alphabet (IPA) that is used in the dictionary to help us learn how to pronounce, read and write English words correctly.

LANGUAGE BANK—In this lesson you learned:

Active words	**Recycled words**	**Passive words**
1. consonant(s)	1. word(s)	1. today
2. beginning	2. new	2. second
3. yesterday	3. learn	3. bear(s)
4. afternoon	4. day(s)	4. bee(s)
5. went-go	5. help	5. beaver(s)
6. we	6. say	6. bat(s)
7. vocabulary	7. different	7. butterfly
8. too	8. nice	8. cow(s)
9. are speaking	9. spring	9. chick(s)
10. clear	10. warm	10. camel(s)
11. voice(s)	11. many	11. crocodile(s)
12. paper(s)	12. flower(s)	12. chameleon(s)
13. collect	13. learn-ed	13. crab(s)
14. improve	14. was hard	14. donkey
15. exercise(s)	15. to hand in	15. duck(s)
16. enjoy-ed	16. spell	16. deer
17. easy	17. problem(s)	17. dove(s)
18. vowel(s)	18. question(s)	18. dolphin(s)
19. there are		19. fawn
20. practise		20. fish

21. express

Expressions: I am so proud of you, it is my pleasure, I am able, make mistakes, all of you, pay attention to . . . . , practice makes perfect

21. frog(s)
22. fox(es)
23. fly
24. flamingo(s)
25. giraffe
26. goose
27. goat(s)
28. grasshopper(s)
29. hen(s)
30. horse(s)
31. jelly fish
32. jackal
33. jaguar(s)
34. koala(s)
35. kangaroo
36. kitten(s)
37. lion(s)
38. leopard(s)
39. llama(s)
40. lamb(s)
41. ladybug(s)
42. mouse
43. monkey(s)
44. mosquito(es)
45. newspaper(s)
46. pig(s)
47. piglet(s)
48. puppy
49. parrot(s)
50. penguin(s)
51. peacock(s)

52. question mark(s)
53. rabbit(s)
54. rooster(s)
55. spider(s)
56. seal(s)
57. swan(s)
58. sheep(s)
59. snail(s)
60. snake(s)
61. turtle(s)
62. turkey
63. vine(s)
64. Valentine
65. whale(s)
66. wolf
67. yoyo(s)
68. yarn

Lesson 3—Short" a", "o" and "æ"

Learning goals: A. Pronunciation of Short **"a"**
B. Pronunciation of Short **"o"**
C. Pronunciation of **"æ"** as in **"at"**

(It is a very nice fall day and the leaves have started to turn yellow and red. Dr. Alba is a little **late** for class. He enters the classroom and apologizes to his students for being late.)

Mr. Knowitall: Good morning everybody. I **am so sorry** that I am late for class today. I was on the phone with Ben`s mother and she **told** me that Ben cannot **come** to school today.

Stephen: (very **concerned**) Is Ben OK, Mr. Knowitall?

Mr. Knowitall: Oh, **no worries**, he **is fine** but he **has a sore throat** today. It is not easy for him to speak. I **am sure** his throat will be better tomorrow and his voice will be back.

51

Paolo: **What** did he do that made him **sick,** Mr. Knowitall?

Mr. Knowitall: I **think** he **played soccer** yesterday afternoon and **then** went home and **drank ice water**. That is **why** he has a sore throat.

Karol: How can we help Ben, Mr. Knowitall?

Mr. Knowitall: I don't think calling him is a good **idea** because Ben cannot speak on the **phone**. You can write a note on paper and **give** it to his mother or you can send him an e-mail.

Monique: That is a very good idea. I like to give Ben some flowers, too.

Ming: I can **take very good notes** in class today and give them to Ben because he can practice the exercises in bed.

Mr. Knowitall: I am so proud of you when I see how you want to help your friend. It is my pleasure to teach such a **wonderful** group of students.

George: I think we can collect some money and buy some fruit like cherries, strawberries, and **apples** for Ben. Does everybody agree?

Karol: That is a wonderful idea, George. (everybody agrees)

George: (changes the discussion to the lesson) Mr. Knowitall, I have a question about the lesson you taught us yesterday because I am not clear. You talked about the International Phonetics Alphabet (IPA) yesterday. **Why** do we need to learn the IPA?

Monique: I wanted to ask **the same** question, Mr. Knowitall. I **hope** you can help **us** understand why IPA is important.

Mr. Knowitall: That is a very good question and the answer is very easy. IPA is an **international system** of **symbols** that helps us learn the **correct pronunciation** of words in English. All the dictionaries write the pronunciation of the words with the International Phonetic Alphabet (IPA) symbols. That is why we need to learn the IPA symbols so we can learn the pronunciation of words we do not know.

Paolo: (excited). Aha, I know. If we want to learn how **to pronounce** a new word, we **must** learn the IPA. That means we will know how to pronounce **even** words that we have not seen before.

Mr. Knowitall: Yes Paolo. You are right.

Stephen: What new things are you going to teach us today, Mr. Knowitall?

Mr. Knowitall: Today we are going to learn how to pronounce short "a", "o" and "æ". Let us practice the correct pronunciation of these sounds with some examples:"a"—cap; "o"—box "æ"—cat;

Monique: Are we going to do some exercises with these sounds, Mr. Knowitall? Exercises help me a lot to learn the correct pronunciation.

Paolo: Me, too. Remember the expression we learned? Practice makes perfect.

Mr. Knowitall: I agree with both of you. **Let us** start the exercises. Remember:

"a"—Word List: had, dad, bad, flag, bag, map, cap, For example **cap**

"æ"—Word List: at, cat, that, an, man, am, jam, For example **cat**

"o"—Word List: top, stop, not, pot, doll, dog, frog, For example **box**

Practice Your Knowledge

Exercise # 1—Vocabulary study

Task 1—Check the meaning of the following words in your dictionary. First, copy the definitions: e. x. **"pronounce"**—say sounds or words in the same way most speakers of a language say them. For example: Mr. Knowitall pronounces the words very clearly.

Task 2—Find the sentence with the same word from the text and copy it or write your own sentence with the new word. Follow the example with the word "pronounce" in task 1.

❑   **late**
Definition ....
Sentence...
❑   **told/tell**
Definition ....
Sentence...
❑   **come**
Definition ....
Sentence...
❑   **concerned**
Definition ....
Sentence...
❑   **what**
Definition ....
Sentence...
❑   **sick**
Definition ....
Sentence...
❑   **think**
Definition ....
Sentence...
❑   **play(ed)**
Definition ....
Sentence...
❑   **soccer**
Definition ....
Sentence...
❑   **then**
Definition ....
Sentence...

❑ **drank/drink**

Definition ....

Sentence ....

❑ **ice**

Definition ....

Sentence ....

❑ **water**

Definition ....

Sentence ....

❑ **why**

Definition ....

Sentence ....

❑ **how**

Definition ....

Sentence ....

❑ **can**

Definition ....

Sentence ....

❑ **phone**

Definition ....

Sentence ....

❑ **give**

Definition ....

Sentence ....

❑ **idea**

Definition ....

Sentence ....

❑ **wonderful**

Definition ....

Sentence ....

❑ **the same**

Definition ....

Sentence ....

❑ **apples**

Definition ....

Sentence ....

❑ **hope**

Definition ....

Sentence ....

❑　　　us

Definition ....

Sentence ....

❑　　　international

Definition ....

Sentence ....

❑　　　system

Definition ....

Sentence ....

❑　　　pronunciation

Definition ....

Sentence ....

❑　　　symbol(s)

Definition ....

Sentence ....

❑　　　correct

Definition ....

Sentence ....

❑　　　to pronounce

Definition ....

Sentence ....

❑　　　must

Definition ....

Sentence ....

❑　　　even

Definition ....

Sentence ....

❑　　　let us

Definition ....

Sentence ....

❑　　　I am sorry

Definition ....

Sentence ....

❑　　　no worries

Definition ....

Sentence ....

❑　　　it is fine

Definition ....

Sentence ....

❏   **have a sore throat**

Definition ....

Sentence...

❏   **I am sure**

Definition ....

Sentence...

❏   **take good notes**

Definition ....

Sentence...

❏   **are/am/ going to ......**

Definition ....

Sentence...

Exercise # 2—Work with a friend (pair work). Read the list of words out loud to your friend. This will help you practice the correct pronunciation of short "<u>a</u>"; "<u>æ</u>" ; "<u>o</u>" ;

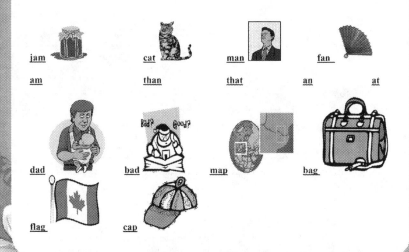

jam   cat   man   fan

am   than   that   an   at

dad   bad   map   bag

flag   cap

top   stop   not   pot

doll   dog   frog   box

Exercise # 3—Find the secret word and practice printing all the words from the list that sound the same:

a)   For example: opt—top, stop, box, pot, dog, frog, doll, not

- mja--
- lold---
- rgof--
- anm---
- anf--
- galf---
- naht--
- na---
- ta--
- ttah--
- adb---
- pma--
- gab---
- apc---
- add---
- tpso--
- tno---
- tpo---
- odg---
- xob---

b) Find the word for each picture and write a sentence with it.

- _ _ _ ....

- _ _ _ ....

- _ _ _ ....

- _ _ _ _ ....

- _ _ _ ....

- _ _ _ ....

- _ _ _ ....

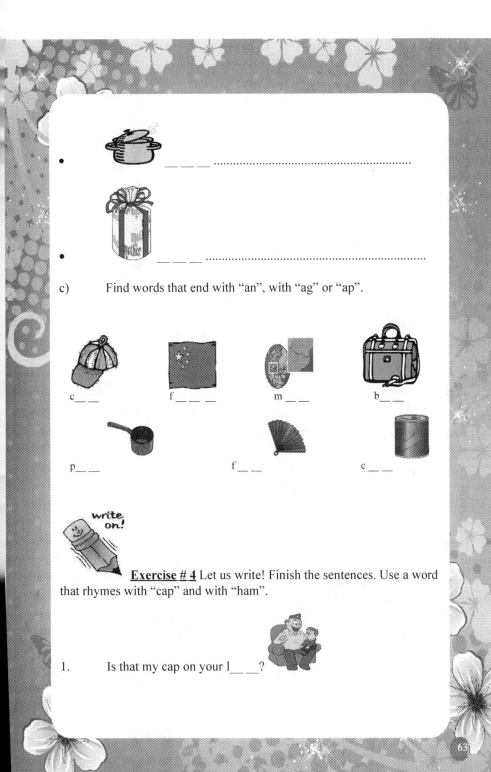

• __ __ __ ....

• __ __ __ ....

c) Find words that end with "an", with "ag" or "ap".

c__ __   f __ __ __   m __ __   b __ __

p__ __   f __ __   c __ __

Exercise # 4 Let us write! Finish the sentences. Use a word that rhymes with "cap" and with "ham".

1.   Is that my cap on your l__ __?

2.   Pam loves ham and Pam loves j__ __ 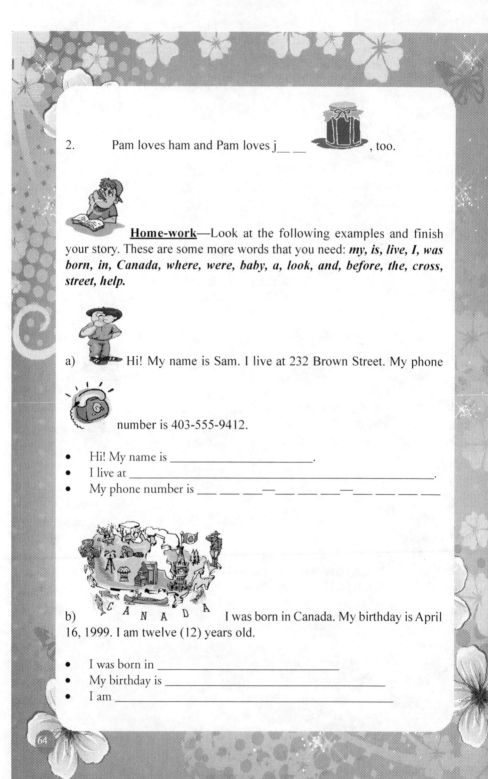, too.

Home-work—Look at the following examples and finish your story. These are some more words that you need: *my, is, live, I, was born, in, Canada, where, were, baby, a, look, and, before, the, cross, street, help.*

a)   Hi! My name is Sam. I live at 232 Brown Street. My phone number is 403-555-9412.

* Hi! My name is _____.
* I live at _____.
* My phone number is ___ ___ ___—___ ___ ___—___ ___ ___ ___

b)   I was born in Canada. My birthday is April 16, 1999. I am twelve (12) years old.

* I was born in _____
* My birthday is _____
* I am _____

c) I stop, look, and listen before I cross the street. Who helps you to cross the street? _____ helps me to cross the street. Draw a picture of you crossing the street.

_____

STUDY TIP-Study everyday—anyone who wants to improve his or her skills in English must set aside some time to study every day. You can read some vocabulary cards at the bus stop, listen to English songs while walking or riding the bus, and watch a TV show in English.

SPOT THE MISTAKE—This book is my English

teacher.

....
....
....

<u>**REMEMBER THIS**</u>—A sentence starts with a capital letter.

<u>**DID YOU KNOW?**</u>—A sentence is a group of words that tells a complete idea.

<u>**LANGUAGE BANK**</u>—In this lesson you learned:

<u>Active words</u>	<u>Recycled words</u>	<u>Passive words</u>
1. late	1. it is	1. start(ed)
2. told/tell	2. nice	2. turn
3. come	3. yellow	3. for example
4. concerned	4. student(s)	4. apologize
5. what	5. today	5. finish
6. sick	6. classroom(s)	6. to end
7. think	7. school(s)	7. verse

8. play(ed)
9. ice
10. water
11. throat(s)
12. why
13. how
14. can
15. phone
16. give
17. idea (s)
18. wonderful
19. the same
20. apple(s)
21. hope
22. us
23. inetrnational
24. system(s)
25. symbol(s)
26. correct
27. pronounce
28. pronunciation
29. must
30. even
31. let us

8. improve
9. voice(s)
10. easy
11. speak
12. yesterday
13. afternoon
14. went
15. home(s)
16. paper(s)
17. because
18. clear
19. flower(s)
20. cherries
21. strawberries
22. too
23. exercise(s)
24. practice
25. collect
26. everybody
27. agree
28. need
29. ask
30. question(s)
31. excited
32. mean
33. sound(s)
34. expression(s)

8. print
9. each
10. pair(s)
11. use
12. rhyme(s)
13. ham
14. bank(s)
15. number(s)
16. dad(s)
17. cap(s)
18. bag(s)
19. map(s)
20. bad
21. top(s)
22. stop
23. not
24. doll(s)
25. frog(s)
26. good

Expressions: I am so sorry, no worries it is fine, have a sore throat, I am sure, take good notes, are/am/ going to . . . .

Lesson 4—My New Country & Ending Sounds

Learning goals: A. Learn new words
B. Learn facts about my new country
C. Learn how to say the ending sounds

(Mr. Knowitall's students have all come to Canada from other countries. They need to learn more about their new country. That is what they are going to discuss in today's class)

Mr. Knowitall: (enters the classroom with a happy face) Good morning everyone. Today we are going to talk about Canada and its **provinces.**

Ben: **Yesterday** I read in a **newspaper** that **some parts** of Canada are **called** provinces and some **areas** are called territories. Is that **right**, Mr. Knowitall?

Mr. Knowitall: Yes, you are right Ben. In Canada we have ten (10) provinces and three (3) territories. Are there any more **questions** about Canada?

Stephen: I **did** some **research** for my Social Studies class and **found out that** a province is not the **same** as a territory.

Paolo: (raises his hand) I **understand** that there is a difference between a province and a territories but **I am not sure** that, too.

Mr. Knowitall: That is OK, Paolo. It is not a **problem**. **Of course** I will **help** you. Canada is **made up of** ten provinces and three territories.

Karol: **I thought** there were only two territories.

Mr. Knowitall: You are right, Karol. That was true but it **changed** in 1999 when the **federal government** made a **decision** to **divide** the Northwest Territory into two parts: the Northwest and Nunavut territories.

 Ming: So, Nunavut is the **new** territory of Canada, right?

Mr. Knowitall: Yes, you are right, Ming. Nunavut has the **largest** area in Canada, 2,000,000 sq. km. **equal** to 1/5 of Canada. Its **capital** is Iqaluit and Nunavut has a **population** of only 4,000 people.

Monique: In the National Geographic **magazine** I read that because Nunavut is **above** the Arctic Circle, winter lasts for nine **months** and the land is **frozen** all the time.

Ming: I read the same magazine and learned that the Nunavut people are called Inuit, **which** in their language means "people".

George: Life must be **difficult** in Nunavut. How do they **move around**?

Mr. Knowitall: **In the old days,** they moved around with **dogsleds** but now they have **snowmobiles** and **airplanes.**

Ben: What do they do for **food** in Nunavut, Mr. Knowitall?

Karol: I have an answer for that from the National Geographic magazine—Inuit **fish** and **hunt** for **their food**. Their food comes from **seals**. They **use** the seal **skin** for **boots**, the seal **meat** for food, and the seal **fat** for **lamp oil**.

Monique: I learned a lot about Nunavut in this lesson but I still have a question—What is the **difference between** a territory and a province?

Mr. Knowitall: That is a very good question, Monique. People in provinces have **constitutional powers** to **govern** their province. Territories, **on the other hand**, are governed by the Parliament of Canada. That is the difference.

Paolo: So, the three territories are: Northwest Territory, Yukon and Nunavut.

Stephen: There are ten provinces, too. They are: British Columbia, Alberta, Manitoba, Saskatchewan, Ontario, Quebec, Nova Scotia, Newfoundland & Labrador, Prince Edward Island, and New Brunswick.

Mr. Knowitall: Thank you. You are right and we have learned something important about Canada. We will continue to learn more in the future lessons. Now we will learn how to **improve** our **vocabulary** by **focusing** on the ending sounds of the words. Let us do the exercises together and that will help us learn more about ending letters and sounds in English.

Practice Your Knowledge

Exercise # 1—Vocabulary study

Task 1—Check the meaning of the following words in your dictionary. Copy the definitions. e. x. **"province"**—is a jurisdiction that receives the power and authority directly from the Constitution Act, 1867. For example—There are ten provinces in Canada.

Task 2—Find the sentence with the same word from the text and copy it or write your own sentence. Follow the example with the first word "province".

❑   **some**

Definition ....

Sentence...

❑ **province(s)**
Definition ....
Sentence ....

❑ **territory**
Definition ....
Sentence ....

❑ **yesterday**
Definition ....
Sentence ....

❑ **question(s)**
Definition ....
Sentence ....

❑ **that**
Definition ....
Sentence ....

❑ **focus**
Definition ....
Sentence ....

❑ **understand**
Definition ....
Sentence ....

❑ **same**
Definition ....
Sentence ....

❑ **research**
Definition ....
Sentence ....

❑ **problem**
Definition ....
Sentence ....

❑ **did/do**
Definition ....
Sentence ....

❑ **decision**
Definition ....
Sentence ....

❑ **federal**
Definition ....
Sentence ....

❑ **government**

Definition ....

Sentence ....

❑ **newspaper**

Definition ....

Sentence ....

❑ **divide(d)**

Definition ....

Sentence ....

❑ **part(s)**

Definition ....

Sentence ....

❑ **area(s)**

Definition ....

Sentence ....

❑ **call (ed)**

Definition ....

Sentence ....

❑ **large(est)**

Definition ....

Sentence ....

❑ **equal**

Definition ....

Sentence ....

❑ **capital**

Definition ....

Sentence ....

❑ **population**

Definition ....

Sentence ....

❑ **above**

Definition ....

Sentence ....

❑ **dogsled(s)**

Definition ....

Sentence ....

❑ **snowmobile(s)**

Definition ....

Sentence ....

❑　　　**to fish**
Definition ....
Sentence ....
❑　　　**to hunt**
Definition ....
Sentence ....
❑　　　**seal(s)**
Definition ....
Sentence ....
❑　　　**boot(s)**
Definition ....
Sentence ....
❑　　　**meat**
Definition ....
Sentence ....
❑　　　**fat**
Definition ....
Sentence ....
❑　　　**think/thought**
Definition ....
Sentence ....
❑　　　**right**
Definition ....
Sentence ....
❑　　　**change(d)**
Definition ....
Sentence ....
❑　　　**new**
Definition ....
Sentence ....
❑　　　**find/found**
Definition ....
Sentence ....
❑　　　**magazine**
Definition ....
Sentence ....
❑　　　**month**
Definition ....
Sentence ....

❑ **frozen**

Definition ....

Sentence ....

❑ **which**

Definition ....

Sentence ....

❑ **difficult**

Definition ....

Sentence ....

❑ **their**

Definition ....

Sentence ....

❑ **difference(s)**

Definition ....

Sentence ....

❑ **between**

Definition ....

Sentence ....

❑ **govern**

Definition ....

Sentence ....

❑ **power(s)**

Definition ....

Sentence ....

❑ **use**

Definition ....

Sentence ....

❑ **improve**

Definition ....

Sentence ....

❑ **constitutional**

Definition ....

Sentence ....

❑ **vocabulary**

Definition ....

Sentence ....

Exercise # 2—Work with a friend (pair work). Say the name of the object in the picture. Write the ending sound.

bird (b)

fish (___)

dog (___)

duck (___)

hear (___)

cat (___)

hen (___)

sheep (___)

monkey (___)

pig (___)

horse (___)

rabbit (___)

table (___)

pizza (___)

tree (___)

chair (___)

book (___)

desk (___)

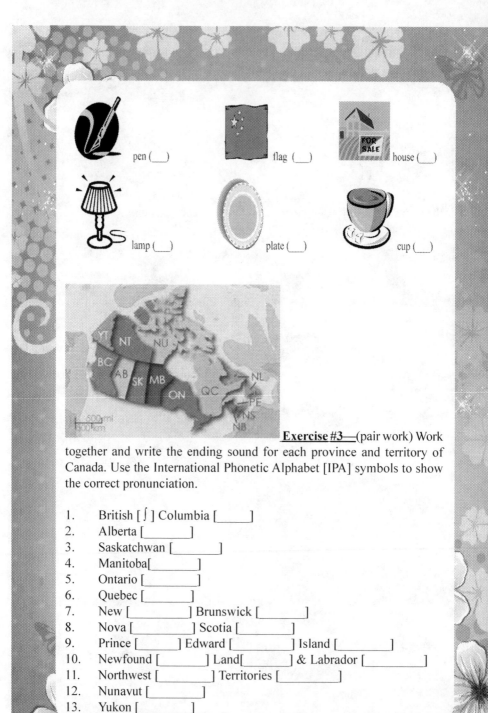

pen (___)

flag (___)

house (___)

lamp (___)

plate (___)

cup (___)

500 mi
500 km

Exercise #3—(pair work) Work together and write the ending sound for each province and territory of Canada. Use the International Phonetic Alphabet [IPA] symbols to show the correct pronunciation.

1. British [∫] Columbia [_____]
2. Alberta [_____]
3. Saskatchwan [_____]
4. Manitoba[_____]
5. Ontario [_____]
6. Quebec [_____]
7. New [_____] Brunswick [_____]
8. Nova [_____] Scotia [_____]
9. Prince [_____] Edward [_____] Island [_____]
10. Newfound [_____] Land[_____] & Labrador [_____]
11. Northwest [_____] Territories [_____]
12. Nunavut [_____]
13. Yukon [_____]

Exercise # 4—Find the secret word and practice writing the word. For example: envicorp—province, province, province. You may choose to write a sentence with the secret word.

- snelbiomwo-_____...................................
  ....
- etnmrnevog-_____..................................
  ....
- adnersnud-_____..................................
  ....
- acrheres-_____...................................
  ....
- yretrirot-_____...................................
  ....

Home-work—Find more information about provinces, territories, and the Arctic Circle. Make a power point presentation with the information and present it in your class.

STUDY TIP—Find a good **Place and Time to Study**—Figuring out a good time and place to do your homework and study is very important. Once you have figured out when to do your homework, the next question is where to do it.

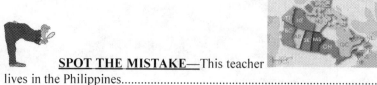

SPOT THE MISTAKE—This teacher lives in the Philippines..
....
....

REMEMBER THIS—A noun is a word for a person, place, thing, or idea.

DID YOU KNOW?—Some nouns are called "common nouns". For example: boy, girl, house, school, car, book, friendship, happiness. Some other nouns are called "proper nouns or names". For example: John, Rita, Toronto, Alberta, Canada.

LANGUAGE BANK—In this lesson you learned:

Active words	**Recycled words**	**Passive words**
1. some	1. come	1. recently

2. province(s)
3. territory
4. yesterday
5. question(s)
6. that
7. focus
8. understand
9. same
10. research
11. problem (s)
12. did/do
13. decision(s)
14. federal
15. government(s)
16. newspaper
17. divide(d)
18. part(s)
19. area(s)
20. call(ed)
21. large(est)
22. equal
23. capital(s)
24. population
25. above
26. dogsled(s)
27. snowmobile(s)
28. to fish
29. to hunt
30. seal(s)
31. meat
32. boot(s)

2. they
3. want
4. learn
5. new
6. country
7. lesson
8. clasroom
9. today
10. anybody
11. go
12. answer(s)
13. thank you
14. spring
15. winter
16. animal
18. people
19. what

2.originally
3. important
4. exercise(s)
5. mistake(s)
6. language(s)
7. bank(s)
8. remember
10. enter
11. any
12. more
13. noun(s)
14. common
15. proper
16. name(s)
17. frienship
18. happiness

33. skin
34. fat
35. help(ed)
36. /think/thought
37. change(d)
38. right
39. vocabulary
40. find/found
41. magazine(s)
42. month(s)
43. frozen
44. which
45. different
46. their
47. improve(d)
48. use(d)
49. airplane(s)
50. food(s)
51. difference
52. between
53. constitutional
54. power(s)
55. govern(ed)

Expressions: of course, I am not sure, made up of, in the old days, on the other hand, move around, lamp oil

Lesson # 5—Facts about Canada & "TH" Sound

Learning goals: A. Learn more about the Arctic
B. Learn how to pronounce **"th"**
C. Learn new words

(Mr. Knowitall starts his class with a **discussion** about more facts on Canadian provinces, territories, and the Arctic Circles which students have **collected** in their research)

Mr. Knowitall: Good morning, everyone. Did you have any questions about the home work? It is **important** to ask me now because today you will be my teachers and I will learn from you more facts about Canada. We will focus on the Arctic Circle in our discussion today.

Ben: Are we all going **to present** today, Mr. Knowitall?

Mr. Knowitall: Yes, Ben. Everyone will present. You can **choose** to make a presentation in your group, to make a drawing or show a PowerPoint based on the facts you have collected about Canada.

Paolo: Thank you for explaining that, Mr. Knowitall. I made a PowerPoint at home but I was not sure if it was OK to present it to the class. I don't like to talk because it is **easy** for me to **show** a PowerPoint and explain.

Stephen: I found some facts from different books in the **library** and I have made some **drawings** of different baby animals that live in the Arctic. Is that OK, Mr. Knowitall?

Mr. Knowitall: I am so **glad** you are choosing to present your **ideas** in different **ways** because different people learn differently. **All kinds of** ways you have chosen to present show that you are all **smart** but you are smart in different ways. That is wonderful. Shall we start with your presentations?

Karol: From my research, I learned that, **although** the Arctic is a very cold place, there are many kinds of animals and fish that **inhabit** that area. The main wildlife in the Arctic is made up of polar bears, whales, and seals, **especially** the **walrus**, which is a kind of seal.

Ming: I found it very **interesting** to read about the ways in which the baby animals live in the Arctic.

Monique: What did you learn about those baby animals, Ming?

Ming: Well, it was **interesting** to learn about the **survival skills** of the walrus. The walrus mother **feeds** the baby with her warm **milk** for two years. To **protect** their babies from the polar bears and killer whales, mothers stay in groups. The baby walrus is called a **calf.**

Mr. Knowitall: Thank you, Ming. That was a very interesting fact. Does anybody want **to add something else?**

George: As I said, I have **prepared** a PowerPoint presentation about the life of the animals in the Arctic. Can I present it?

Mr. Knowitall: Of course, we are very happy **to listen** to your presentation, George.

George: (starts his presentation by projecting the slides on the screen) Well, I found an interesting fact about the seals, not the walrus.

Different from the walrus, the seal is a mother only for ten days. After that, the mother seal **leaves** her pups to **take care of** themselves.

Karol: Poor babies. They must be very unhappy.

George: It is very interesting because **at first**, they **cry** for their mother. When they understand that she is not coming, they swim **deep** into the **sea**. This helps them; they learn how to swim and hunt themselves.

Ben: I researched the baby polar bears. Although polar bears eat meat, their babies **are born** without teeth. Also, for the first **month** they cannot see, hear, or walk. The mother bear must teach everything to her **cubs.**

Mr. Knowitall: All these facts are every interesting. We have learned so many things about the wildlife in the Arctic. I am very happy with the ways you are improving your English skills. Also, I am proud to see how you are using research to learn more about your new country. Thank you and see you next time.

Practice Your Knowledge

Exercise # 1—Vocabulary study.

Task 1—Check the meaning of the following words in your dictionary. Copy the definitions. e. x. **"library"**—the building or room where we put all the books. Mr. Knowitall has a big library.

Task 2—Find the sentence with the same word from the text and copy it or write your own sentence. Follow the example with the word "library".

❑   **discussion(s)**
Definition ....
Sentence...
❑   **collect**
Definition ....
Sentence...
❑   **important**
Definition ....
Sentence...
❑   **to present**
Definition ....
Sentence...
❑   **easy**
Definition ....
Sentence...

❑ **show**

Definition ....

Sentence ....

❑ **drawing(s)**

Definition ....

Sentence ....

❑ **glad**

Definition ....

Sentence ....

❑ **choose**

Definition ....

Sentence ....

❑ **idea(s)**

Definition ....

Sentence ....

❑ **smart**

Definition ....

Sentence ....

❑ **although**

Definition ....

Sentence ....

❑ **inhabit**

Definition ....

Sentence ....

❑ **way(s)**

Definition ....

Sentence ....

❑ **interesting**

Definition ....

Sentence ....

❑ **survival**

Definition ....

Sentence ....

❑ **skill(s)**

Definition ....

Sentence ....

❑ **walrus**

Definition ....

Sentence ....

❑   **feed**

Definition ....

Sentence ....

❑   **protect**

Definition ....

Sentence ....

❑   **add**

Definition ....

Sentence ....

❑   **prepare**

Definition ....

Sentence ....

❑   **something**

Definition ....

Sentence ....

❑   **listen**

Definition ....

Sentence ....

❑   **leave**

Definition ....

Sentence ....

❑   **deep**

Definition ....

Sentence ....

❑   **sea**

Definition ....

Sentence ....

❑   **cry**

Definition ....

Sentence ....

❑   **(to be) born**

Definition ....

Sentence ....

❑   **also**

Definition ....

Sentence ....

❑   **month(s)**

Definition ....

Sentence ....

❑   **cub(s)**
Definition ....
Sentence ....

Exercise # 2—It is difficult to learn the correct pronunciation of the [θ] and the [ð] sounds. Work with a friend (pair work), say the word and then write it 5-10 times until you learn the difference in the pronunciation of the [θ] and the [ð] sounds. Look at the example—thank thank thank thank thank thank thank thank thank

A.
think—['thiŋk]_____
thing—[θɪŋ]_____
thin—[θɪn]_____
thick—[θɪk]_____
bath—[bæθ]_____
path—[pæθ]_____
month—[mʌnθ]_____
math—[mæθ]_____

B.
the—[ðə]_____
then—[ðen]_____
them—[ðem]_____
they—[ðeɪ]_____
these—[ði:z]_____
those—[ðoʊz]_____
than—[ðæn]_____
there—[ðeə(r)]_____
this—[ðɪs]_____
that—[ðæt]_____
with—[wɪð]_____

Exercise #3—Practice the correct pronunciation of "the"-words. Read the sentences to your friend. Write the sentences in your notebook.

This is a thin thing.

These are thin things, too.

I cannot stop thinking about them.

Thank you for all these things.

Exercise # 4—Find the secret word and practice writing the word. Write a sentence with the discovered secret word. For example: ionsuscsdi—discussion, discussion, discussion, discussion, discussion, discussion, discussion—We had a good discussion in class today.

- nttaoripm-_____..

- uhgohtla-_____...
- nigestterni-_____..
- usrawl-_____..
- ectortp-_____..

Home-work—Find the names of the parents of these baby animals. Read the sentences. Look at the pictures and fill in the blanks with one of the words from the list.

dog   horse   goose   cat   pig   hen   cow

A foal is a baby _____.

A calf is a baby _____.

A puppy is a baby _____.

A piglet is a baby _____.

A chick is a baby _____.

A gosling is a baby _____.

A kitten is a baby _____.

STUDY TIP—Learn how to do skimming to improve your reading skills. What is **Skimming**?—It is a reading skill: when you read, focus on the title, the author and the source. Also, look for names of people, places, ideas, numbers, and words like therefore, moreover, instead of before you make a decision to keep reading.

SPOT THE MISTAKE—This is a baby walrus and he is swimming in the deep sea...
....
....
....

REMEMBER THIS—Many plural nouns are formed by adding "s" to the singular nouns. Some plural nouns are formed by adding "es" to the singular nouns. There are some nouns that do not follow these rules at all.

DID YOU KNOW?—There are five vowels in the English alphabet. They are a, e, i, o, u. Sometimes "y" is considered a vowel. Vowels can form long or short sounds.

LANGUAGE BANK—In this lesson you learned:

Active words	Recycled words	Passive words
1. discussion(s)	1. province	1. project
2. collect	2. territory	2. slide(s)
3. important	3. research	3. screen(s)

4. to present
5. library
6. easy
7. to show
8. drawing(s)
9. glad
10. choose
11. idea(s)
12. smart
13. althought
14. inhabit
15. way(s)
16. interesting
17. survival
18. skill(s)
19. walrus
20. feed
21. protect
22. add
23. prepare
24. something
25. listen
26. leave
27. deep
28. sea
29. cry
30. are born
31. also
32. month(s)
33. cub(s)

4. start
5. fact
6. their
7. questions
8. homework
9. today
10. focus
11. everyone
12. was sure
13. found
14. different
15. some
16. animal(s)
17. area
18. is made up of
19. warm
20. want
21. anybody
22. of course

4. plural
5. form
6. singular
7. vowel(s)
8. consider
9. notebook(s)
10. powerpoint
11. presentation
12. make sure
13. cover slide
14. at least

Expressions: all kinds of, take care of, at first

Lesson 6—Words from Immigrants &|
Confusing Letters

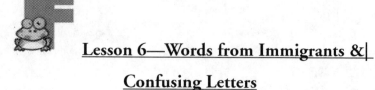

Learning goals: A. Understand confusing letters
B. Learn the origin of the words
C. Words brought by immigrants

(Students who are learning English usually are **immigrants** to this country and they need to learn both the sounds and the words of the new language. Also, it is interesting for them to learn that some of the English words were **brought** into the English language by immigrants.)

Mr. Knowitall: Good morning, everyone. Today our discussion will focus on two **main** **topics**: immigrants' **contributions** to the English language and some problems with **confusing** letters and sounds in English.

Ben: I do not know of any **special** contributions that immigrants have given to the English language. English is so different from our first language. Is immigration even important to this country?

Stephen: Of course, immigration is important. In our Social Studies class we have learned that both America and Canada need **to bring** immigrants to their countries because their population is getting older every day.

Paolo: On the other hand, immigrants need to leave their countries to find **better employment**, better education for their children, and more freedom. Immigrants must learn English in the new country but they, also, use some words from their first language and sometimes those words **become** part of the English language.

Mr. Knowitall: You are **making a very good point**, Paolo. Learning English is a big **responsibility** because it is the language of your new country but **sometimes** words from other languages **enrich** English, too. The word `hamburger`` is a very good **example**. Do you know the **history** of this word?

Karol: I know the story; that is **easy**—a hamburger is **made out of ham**.

Mr. Knowitall: That may be the way we **think,** Karol, but, in fact, it is not **true**. The hamburger is not made out of ham. This word was brought to English by immigrants and it is **connected** to the **seaport** town of Hamburg, Germany.

Ming: I know that story, too. Can I **share** it, Mr.Knowitall?

Mr. Knowitall: I am glad you know that story, Ming. Please, share it with your friends.

Ming: In 1700s, many **Europeans** started to immigrate to the New World, America and Canada. **At that time**, immigrants went to the seaport of Hamburg, Germany to take a ship to **travel** to North America. The ships were part of the Hamburg-America ship **line** and the main **food** people in the ship **ate** were hamburgers—a **patty** of **ground meat** that is **grilled** and **served** in a **bun**.

Monique: I **understand** it, German immigrants brought the word ``hamburger`` to English. This is very interesting because the word does not **exist** in the German language but it was **formed** by the immigrants in Hamburg-America line ships and is used in English every day.

Mr. Knowitall: You are both right. After that, the word ``hamburger`` **became** more **popular** with **fast** food restaurants opening all over the world.

George: It sounds like the same story as when Italian immigrants brought the word ``pizza`` into English. It is interesting; immigrants have to learn English but they, also, have brought some words into the English language.

Monique: Yes, but for me that does not make it easier to learn English. Especially, there are some words that look the same but sound different. That makes reading and writing very difficult for me.

Mr. Knowitall: I know that learning English is not easy. **Which** letters are difficult for you, Monique?

Monique: My first language is Arabic and our letters are not the same as the English alphabet. So, I **confuse** some pairs of letters in English. For example: p-q, m-n, v-u, b-d, P-R.

Paolo: I have some problems with the sounds, Mr. Knowitall. Some of the English sounds do not exist in my first language and it is difficult for me to **pronounce** them. I confuse them. For example: th-s, r—l, p-v.

Mr. Knowitall: That is very important for me to know and I will help you. We will do some exercises that will help you learn those letters and sounds. Let us start working with exercises.

Practice Your Knowledge

write on!

Exercise # 1—Vocabulary study.

Task 1—Check the meaning of the following words in your dictionary. Copy the definitions e. x. **"immigrant"**—a newcomer to a country. I am an immigrant in this country.

Task 2—Find the sentence with the same word from the text and copy it or write your own sentence.

❏   **main**
Definition ....

Sentence...
❑   **topic(s)**
Definition ....
Sentence...
❑   **bring (brought)**
Definition ....
Sentence...
❑   **contribution(s)**
Definition ....
Sentence...
❑   **special**
Definition ....
Sentence...
❑   **confusing**
Definition ....
Sentence...
❑   **better(good)**
Definition ....
Sentence...
❑   **employment**
Definition ....
Sentence...
❑   **responsibility**
Definition ....
Sentence...
❑   **sometimes**
Definition ....
Sentence...
❑   **enrich**
Definition ....
Sentence...
❑   **example**
Definition ....
Sentence...
❑   **history**
Definition ....
Sentence...

❑ **easy**

Definition ....

Sentence ....

❑ **ham**

Definition ....

Sentence ....

❑ **think**

Definition ....

Sentence ....

❑ **true**

Definition ....

Sentence ....

❑ **connected**

Definition ....

Sentence ....

❑ **seaport(s)**

Definition ....

Sentence ....

❑ **share**

Definition ....

Sentence ....

❑ **European(s)**

Definition ....

Sentence ....

❑ **line(s)**

Definition ....

Sentence ....

❑ **food**

Definition ....

Sentence ....

❑ **ate(eat)**

Definition ....

Sentence ....

❑ **patty**

Definition ....

Sentence ....

❑ **grill**

Definition ....

Sentence ....

❑　　serve

Definition ....

Sentence...

❑　　bun(s)

Definition ....

Sentence...

❑　　understand

Definition ....

Sentence...

❑　　exist

Definition ....

Sentence...

❑　　to form

Definition ....

Sentence...

❑　　become

Definition ....

Sentence...

❑　　popular

Definition ....

Sentence...

❑　　fast

Definition ....

Sentence...

❑　　which

Definition ....

Sentence...

❑　　pronounce

Definition ....

Sentence...

write on!

Exercise # 2—Look at these confusing pairs of letters. Which letters do not belong inside the shape? Circle those letters.

Exercise # 3—Work with a friend (pair work) and follow directions.

❖   Look at the word—BED-. Colour the "d" sound in blue and the "b" sound in yellow.

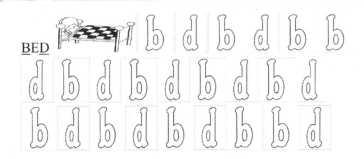

BED

❖   Look at the words "prince" and "queen". Colour the "p" sound in yellow and the "q" sound in red.

prince and queen

❖   Look at the words "ice cream" and "jelly". Colour the "i" sound in brown and the "j" sound in yellow.

ice cream and jelly

❖ The letter "m" has two humps, the letter "n" has only one hump. Colour the "m" sound in green and the "n" sound in brown.

two humps

one hump

❖ Look at the words "violin" and "umbrella". Colour the "v" sound in yellow and the "u" sound in blue.

violin   umbrella

Exercise # 4—Find the secret word and write a sentence with it.

❖ entmyoemlp-_____ ....
....
❖ ilytbiisrenops-_____ ....
....
❖ leamxep-_____ ....
....
❖ ortpaes-_____ ....
....
❖ adntserdun-_____ ....
....

Home-work—Search and find five English words that come from other languages. Write a sentence with each word.

1. ....
....
2. ....
....
3. ....
....
4. ....
....
5. ....
....

STUDY TIP—Reading is very important to improve your English and learn about the new culture. You must learn to read with a purpose. Before you start reading, think of the purpose you have for the reading.

SPOT THE MISTAKE—This ship is in another seaport and will arrive to Canada today.....................................

....

....

....

REMEMBER THIS—A verb is the action word in a sentence. It shows what the subject of the sentence is doing.

DID YOU KNOW?—When we add a silent "e" at the end of a word, the vowel in the word changes from short to long vowel. This changes the meaning of the word, too. For example, look at the words: "tap" and "tape"; "cap" and "cape".

LANGUAGE BANK—In this lesson you learned:

Active words	Recycled words	Passive words
1. immigrant(s)	1. learn	1. usually
2. main	2. sound(s)	2. need
3. topic(s)	3. both	3. secret(s)
4. bring(brought)	4. word(s)	4. violin(s)
5. contribution(s)	5. glad	5. hump(s)
6. special	6. some	6. ice cream
7. confusing	7. know	7. jelly
8. good(better)	8. different	8. prince(s)
9. employment	9. language(s)	9. queen(s)
10. become	10. discussion(s)	10. circle(s)
11. responsibility	11. focus	11. belong
12. sometimes	12. problem(s)	12. shape(s)
13. enrich	13. important	13. culture(s)
14. example(s)	14. of course	14. purpose(s)
15. history	15. population	15. arrive
16. easy	16. leave	
17. ham	17. part(s)	
18. think	18. way(s)	

19. true
20. connected
21. seaport(s)
22. share
23. European(s)
24. line(s)
25. food
26. ate(eat)
27. patty
28. grill
29. serve
30. bun(s)
31. understand
32. exist
33. to form
34. popular
35. fast
36. which
37. confuse
38. pronounce

19. town(s)
20. travel
21. right

Expressions: getting older, on the other hand, make appoint, made out of, in fact, at that time, ground beef.

Check Your Knowledge

Let us review our knowledge

Exercise # 1: Pronounce the word for the object in the picture. Write **the beginning sound**. Get extra points if you can write all the letters of the word.

Exercise #2—Write the letters that are missing in the English alphabet.

a	__	c	__	__	f	
__	h	__	j	__	l	
m	__	o	__	q	__	s
t	__	v	__			

Score --------/11

Exercise # 3-Look at these pairs of confusing letters. Which letters do not belong in the group? Circle the letters that do not belong.

m n m n h m

h n m n m h h n

m n h m n n m n

u v w y u v

u v u v u v w u v

w u v w v w u

p q p b p q p q

q b q q p q q q p

b q b q p q p q b

Score --------/15

Exercise # 4-Write the letter that comes after each letter of the alphabet.

m _____   q _____   n _____   p _____   g _____   r _____

x _____   u _____   c _____   s _____   d _____   f _____

w _____   h _____   y _____   k _____   o _____   i _____

Score --------/18

Exercise # 5-Find the beginning sound and complete the following words.

__ird	__ear	__up	__uck	__ish	__en
__orse	__onkey	__ig	__ook	__air	__up
__esk	__lag	__ouse	__amp	__en	__izza
__late	__able	__ree	__un	__lag	__ox

Score --------/24

Exercise #6-Write the ending sound for each of the following word and pronounce them correctly.

boo__   chai__   cu__   des__   dru__   fa__   fla__   ja__   lam__ pe___ su___ boo___ shee___ tre___ tabl___ pi___ hors___ do___

Score -------/9

Exercise # 7—Look these words; pay special attention to "the" sound. Is the sound a [θ]sound or a [ð]sound? Write the pronunciation of each word in IPA alphabet.

bath [   ]   with [   ]   month [   ]   these [   ]   path [   ]
this [   ]   math [   ]   thin [   ]   then [   ]   them [   ]
thing [   ]   thank [   ]   there [   ]   thick [   ]   they [   ]
than [   ]   those [   ]   math [   ]   this [   ]   that [   ]

Score -------/10

Exercise # 8—Choose the best word for each sentence.

☐   He is a _____ (jam, man)
☐   I have a _____ (jam, crab)
☐   It is in the _____ (fan, bag)
☐   The crab is not in the _____ (fan, bag)
☐   The book is in the _____ (bag, ham)

Score -------/5

Score -------/100

Correct mistakes.

Write down your mistakes and look at them. Look at each word that you missed and write it at home again:

Lesson 7—Animal World & Short and Long Vowel "U"

Learning goals: A. Learn about animals and words

B. Short vowel "**u**"

C. Long vowel "**u**"

(When spring comes, days get warmer. There are a lot of animals running in the fields at the farm and there are different **insects**, too. Students are learning about the farm and the animals in their **science** class. So, the discussion in this class focuses on animals and insects.)

Mr. Knowitall: What a beautiful **weather** we are having these days. The temperature is warm and the animals and insects are everywhere.

Monique: Last week I visited a farm. It was so beautiful to see the animals eating grass outside in the fields.

Ben: We have studied facts about animals and insects in our science class. Some of the words in that lesson were very difficult for me. Can we learn some words about the animals, insects, and the farm, Mr. Knowitall?

Mr. Knowitall: That is a very interesting topic, Ben. It will be very interesting to discuss about the animals, insects and the farm. Does anybody know any stories about animals?

Stephen: (tells his story) Last week, my mother and I **went** to the animal **shelter** because we wanted to get a **pet**. The animal shelter is the place where dogs and cats stay **until** people **adopt** them. There are other animals there, too. We **picked out** a beautiful orange and brown cat. We gave our new cat a name. His name is Puffy.

Paolo: (tells another story) My grandmother lives in a farm. She has many animals. In summer I go to my grandmother's farm. I like her animals. She has a big, brown, and white cow. The cow gives us milk and

I **drink** milk every the morning. There are many **goats** in the farm. Goats give us milk, too. My grandmother, also, has a small, pink pig. It eats a lot and is **always dirty** because he wants to play in the **mud**.

 Karol: It **must** be so interesting in the farm, Paolo. I have **never** seen a farm. The **lambs** must be beautiful. What do you eat when you are at the farm, Paolo? There must be a lot of **fresh food** and vegetables there.

Paolo: (thinks) Let me see. When I am in the farm, I have eggs for **breakfast**. **Sometimes** they are hen eggs and sometimes **duck** eggs. I like them very much. Our **hen** has a nice family (laughs): her husband—Mr. **Rooster** and her three chickens. Our ducks have no **ducklings** this **year**.

Mr. Knowitall: Those are very interesting stories. Thank you. Does anybody want to **share** other information about animals or insects?

Ming: I know that some animals are very smart. For example, pets are smart and they become a very special part of our **family**.

George: I like **bees** , **butterflies** , and **ladybugs**

. But I do not think **worms** are insects.

Ben: I like bees because they give us **honey**. They work hard. Bees have **antennas** that show them the direction to fly.

Karol: I like butterflies, too, because they are **pretty** and have beautiful **wings** with many colours.

Monique: I like animals and insects, too, but I do not like one insect which is the biggest **pest** of all (laughs).

Mr. Knowitall: Can anybody guess which insect Monique does not like? That little insect can **ruin** an interesting **camping trip** in the **woods** in summer.

Paolo: I think that insect is a **mosquito**. Is that right, Monique?

Monique: Yes, you are right, Paolo. Does anybody know any facts about mosquitoes?

Stephen: I do. I have read that only the **female** mosquitoes **bite,** boys do not bite (laughs). Female mosquitoes drink our **blood** to get the **protein** they need to make their eggs. One little bite on your arm can **produce** 50-100 eggs.

Carol: I knew that the **male** mosquito does not bite; it **feeds** only on plant juices. You can **prevent** mosquitoes from biting you by not **wearing** dark colours, for example blue jeans. Also, do not use **perfume** or body lotion because mosquitoes like the good smell.

Mr. Knowitall: I like your discussion about animals and insects today. You **remember** a lot of information from your science class. That shows that you pay very good attention to your classes. We have learned many words today and now you can **take a break**. Let us do the exercises after the break.

Practice Your Knowledge

<u>Exercise # 1</u>—Vocabulary study

Task 1—Check the meaning of the following words in your dictionary. Copy the definitions. e. x. **"insect"**—a small creature that crawls or flies and sometimes bites to get protein for its eggs. There are more than a million kinds of insects including flies, mosquitoes, bees etc.

Task 2—Find the sentence with the same word from the text and copy it or write your own sentence. Follow the example with the word "insect".

❑ **insect(s)**
Definition ....
Sentence..
❑ **science**
Definition ....
Sentence..
❑ **weather**
Definition ....
Sentence..
❑ **go/went**
Definition ....
Sentence..
❑ **shelter(s)**
Definition ....
Sentence..

❑ **pet(s)**
Definition ....
Sentence ....
❑ **until**
Definition ....
Sentence ....
❑ **adopt**
Definition ....
Sentence ....
❑ **milk**
Definition ....
Sentence ....
❑ **drink**
Definition ....
Sentence ....
❑ **goat(s)**
Definition ....
Sentence ....
❑ **always**
Definition ....
Sentence ....
❑ **dirty**
Definition ....
Sentence ....
❑ **mud**
Definition ....
Sentence ....
❑ **must**
Definition ....
Sentence ....
❑ **never**
Definition ....
Sentence ....
❑ **lamb(s)**
Definition ....
Sentence ....
❑ **breakfast**
Definition ....
Sentence ....

❑ **sometimes**

Definition ....

Sentence ....

❑ **duck(s)**

Definition ....

Sentence ....

❑ **hen(s)**

Definition ....

Sentence ....

❑ **rooster(s)**

Definition ....

Sentence ....

❑ **duckling**

Definition ....

Sentence ....

❑ **year(s)**

Definition ....

Sentence ....

❑ **share**

Definition ....

Sentence ....

❑ **family**

Definition ....

Sentence ....

❑ **bee(s)**

Definition ....

Sentence ....

❑ **butterfly**

Definition ....

Sentence ....

❑ **ladybug(s)**

Definition ....

Sentence ....

❑ **worm(s)**

Definition ....

Sentence ....

❑ **honey**

Definition ....

Sentence ....

❑ **antenna(s)**

Definition ....

Sentence ....

❑ **wing(s)**

Definition ....

Sentence ....

❑ **pretty**

Definition ....

Sentence ....

❑ **woods**

Definition ....

Sentence ....

❑ **mosquito(s)**

Definition ....

Sentence ....

❑ **female(s)**

Definition ....

Sentence ....

❑ **male(s)**

Definition ....

Sentence ....

❑ **bite**

Definition ....

Sentence ....

❑ **blood**

Definition ....

Sentence ....

❑ **protein**

Definition ....

Sentence ....

❑ **produce**

Definition ....

Sentence ....

❑ **feed**

Definition ....

Sentence ....

❑ **prevent**

Definition ....

Sentence ....

❑　　**perfume**

Definition ....

Sentence...

Exercise # 2—Work with a friend (pair work). Say and write the name of the insect in the picture; read the description, and draw the insect.

* Write the word for this insect: _____

o draw the insect and colour it: an oval shape body; oval shape wings; round eyes.

_____

* Write the word for this insect: _____

o draw the insect and color it: one oval shape body; 2 wings with many angles; 2 smaller wings; draw small and big circles on the wings; 2 round eyes; 2 curved antennas.

_____

* Write the word for this insect: _____

o   draw the insects and color it: a big, round body; a triangle inside the body: big and small circles on the body; half a circle for the head; 2 round eyes; 2 curved antennas.

_____

•   Write the word for this creature: _____

o   draw a worm and color it: 2 long, wavy lines for the body; curves inside the body.

_____

Exercise # 3—Find the secret word and write a sentence with it.

•   yfltertbu_____ -------------------------------

•   ucedpro_____ -------------------------------

•   fsatkaebr _____ -------------------------------

•   ecensic _____ -------------------------------

•   uiqtoosm_____ -------------------------------

Exercise # 4—Read the following list of words out loud. The "u" in these words is a short vowel. Write the correct pronunciation of the word using the International Phonetic Alphabet (IPA).

hug[   ]   bug[   ]   run[   ]   sun[   ]

fun[   ]   duck[   ]   truck[   ]   mug[   ]

•   Practice writing all the words above: Example: hug hug hug hug hug hug hug hug hug hug

bug--
run--
sun--
fun--
duck--
truck--
mug---

•   Write the word for each picture (see the words above).

Exercise # 5—Let's write! These are more words that you need to complete this task: **go, school, to, we, is, it, at, picture, finish**

I go to School number 42. It is on Flag Street. When the sun comes up, I drink a mug of milk and I run to school. We have fun at school.

Draw a picture of your school and finish the sentences to describe your school.

_____

I go to _____ School. It is on _____ . I am in grade _____ . In the morning, I drink a _____

and then _____ . I have a lot of _____ at school.

Homework: Write one sentence with each word you see in the picture and you learned in Lesson 7.

_____

Study

STUDY TIP—Learn the definitions of the words. Many pairs of words sound the same or nearly the same, but each has a different meaning. Those words can be confusing and are called—**homophones**—Words like these can be easily confused with each other. You must be careful to learn the definition and use the correct word. If not, you may mean something and express something that is very different. E.x. there—their, hear-here, gone-gun.

SPOT THE MISTAKE—This insect bites people and drinks their blood to get protein to make its eggs....................

....
....
....

REMEMBER THIS-A sentence begins with a capital letter and ends with a period.

DID YOU KNOW? Two words that share the same meaning are synonyms.

LANGUAGE BANK—In this lesson you learned:

Active words	**Recycled words**	**Passive words**
1. insect(s)	1. discussion	1. dictionary
2. science	2. focus	2. check

3. weather
4. go-went
5. shelter(s)
6. pet
7. until
8. adopt
9. milk
10. drink
11. goat(s)
12. always
13. dirty
14. mud
15. must
16. never
17. lamb(s)
18. breakfast
19. sometimes
20. duck(s)
21. hen(s)
22. rooster(s)
23. share
24. duckling(s)
25. year(s)
26. family
27. bee(s)
28. butterfly
29. ladybug(s)
30. worm(s)
31. honey
32. antenna(s)
33. wing(s)

3. animal(s)
4. interesting
5. smart
6. understand
7. special
8. which
9. form
10. cow(s)
11. like
12. too
13. anybody
14. little
15. summer
16. think
17. anything
18. know
19. read
20. right
21. drink
22. because
23. excercise(s)
24. warm
25. a lot of
26. beautiful
27. grass
28. eat
29. field(s)
30. class(es)
31. word(s)
32. discuss
33. about

3. following
4. copy
5. description
6. secret(s)
7. hug(s)
8. mug(s)
9. bug(s)
10. truck(s)
11. definition(s)
12. nearly
13. mean
14. express
15. different
16. period
17. synonym(s)

Expressions: pick out, fresh food, take a break, camping trip

34. pretty
35. woods
36. mosquito(s)
37. female(s)
38. bite
39. protein
40. produce
41. male
42. feed on
43. prevent
43. perfume
44. ruin

34. story
35. play
36. smell
37. confused
38. something

Lesson 8—Celebrations

& Short Vowel "I"

Learning goals: A. Learn about holidays
B. Cultural information
C. Learn how to pronounce **"i"**

(It is the day before Halloween and students have many questions for Mr. Knowitall. Their main questions are about **holidays** and different **celebrations** in the new country.)

Mr. Knowitall: Good morning, folks. Here we come **to celebrate** another **glorious** fall day. Have you **noticed** the weather these days and the **marvelous** change of colours in the trees?

Ben: Yes, those colours are really marvelous. Fall is a beautiful season and I like it very much.

Stephen: All this **week** I have watched **television** and they talk about a special celebration that is coming at the end of **October**.

Paolo: You are right; they sometimes show some **scary** people with blood coming down from their eyes.

Mr. Knowitall: Yes, they are talking about a Canadian celebration called Halloween. On Halloween Night, children go **trick-or-treating** in the **neighbourhoods**. They are **dressed up** like **ghosts** and other **characters** from movies or stories.

Karol: It sounds like a **silly** celebration. Why do they dress up like ghosts?

Ming: I read about that in a book at the library. Some people think that this popular celebration comes from England. On All Souls Day, **poor** people went to **rich** houses and **promised** that they will **pray** for **their dead** if the rich people gave them food.

Mr. Knowitall: It is a tradition that a **jack-o-lantern** is put **in front of** the house to tell children that they can come in for **treats**. Some people believe that Halloween helps to connect living people and dead people.

Monique: It may be a fun night for children and they can dress up and get a lot of **candy** but this celebration is not for me as I am scared of ghosts and blood. I am **thankful** we do not have this celebration in my country.

Ming: Some of the celebrations here are the same as in my country.

Mr. Knowitall: You are right, Ming. Different countries share some celebrations. For example, many countries celebrate the New Year, some celebrate Christmas, and some others celebrate Eid-al-Fitr or Hanukkah.

Ben: Many families **decorate** green trees before Christmas and the New Year. There are many kinds of **ornaments** on the green tree.

Usually there is a yellow star at the top of the tree. The tree must be big and green and it **needs** many lights and ornaments.

Monique: There are a lot of **presents under** the tree, too. Boys' presents have wavy lines or stars on blue or green paper. Girls' presents are **tied** with big red **bows.**

George: People say that the night before Christmas, Santa Claus **comes** to children's house **making sure** that presents will be **ready** before the children **wake up**.

Karol: Sometimes presents go under the tree and sometimes they go in **stockings** with children's name on them. Girls' stockings have some flowers on them. Boys' stockings have small balls painted on them.

George: Another **popular** celebration is the birthday party.

Mr. Knowitall: Yes, of course. Many families celebrate birthdays as a happy event for their family.

Paolo: I went to a friend's birthday party last week, it was **lovely**. She **turned** sixteen years old. She had a bright, red and blue dress on at her birthday party. Her mother had made a **delicious** lemon cake with sixteen candles on it. My friend got many presents. The biggest one was from her parents.

Mr. Knowitall: I am happy you had that **experience**, Paolo. That sounds like a **typical** birthday party. I am sure you will have more such experiences in the future. Now, let us work with some of the words that we learned today.

Practice Your Knowledge

write on!

<u>Exercise # 1</u>—Vocabulary study

Task 1—Check the meaning of the following words in your dictionary. Copy the definitions. e. x. **"celebration"**—to show happiness that something good has happened by doing such things as eating or playing music. I participated in a great celebration for my sister's graduation.

Task 2—Find the sentence with the same word from the text and copy it or write your own sentence. Follow the example with the word "celebration".

❑   **holiday(s)**

Definition ....

Sentence ....

❑   **celebrate**

Definition ....

Sentence ....

❑   **glorious**

Definition ....

Sentence ....

❑   **notice**

Definition ....

Sentence ....

❑   **marvelous**

Definition ....

Sentence ....

❑   **October**

Definition ....

Sentence ....

❑   **television**

Definition ....

Sentence ....

❑   **week**

Definition ....

Sentence ....

❑   **scary**

Definition ....

Sentence ....

❑   **neighbourhood**

Definition ....

Sentence ....

❑   **character(s)**

Definition ....

Sentence ....

❑   **ghost(s)**

Definition ....

Sentence ....

❑   **silly**

Definition ....

Sentence ....

❑   **poor**

Definition ....

Sentence ....

❑   **rich**

Definition ....

Sentence ....

❑   **promise(s)**

Definition ....

Sentence ....

❑   **the dead**

Definition ....

Sentence ....

❑   **pray**

Definition ....

Sentence ....

❑   **treat(s)**

Definition ....

Sentence ....

❑   **candy**

Definition ....

Sentence ....

❑   **thankful**

Definition ....

Sentence ....

❑   **decorate**

Definition ....

Sentence ....

❑   **ornament(s)**

Definition ....

Sentence ....

❑   **need**

Definition ....

Sentence ....

❑   **under**

Definition ....

Sentence ....

❑   **tie**

Definition ....

Sentence ....

❑ **bow**

Definition ....

Sentence ....

❑ **come**

Definition ....

Sentence ....

❑ **present(s)**

Definition ....

Sentence ....

❑ **ready**

Definition ....

Sentence ....

❑ **stocking(s)**

Definition ....

Sentence ....

❑ **popular**

Definition ....

Sentence ....

❑ **lovely**

Definition ....

Sentence ....

❑ **turned**

Definition ....

Sentence ....

❑ **delicious**

Definition ....

Sentence ....

❑ **experience**

Definition ....

Sentence ....

❑ **typical**

Definition ....

Sentence ....

Exercise # 2—Here are some pictures that you can choose to colour. See if you can finish and colour one of the following drawings. Write your story after you finish colouring the picture. You can choose to work with picture (a), (b) or (c).

a) The picture of Eric's house on Christmas day, colour it and write your story. Use many words you learned in this lesson.

Write your story --

----

b)   Cindy drew a picture of herself at her birthday party but it is not
     finished yet. You are going to finish it for her. Cindy has blue eyes
     and wears a red ribbon around her ponytail. Draw and color the
     two things we just talked about. Also, she is wearing a blue blouse.
     Her skirt is red. Cindy's shoes are brown. Her shoelaces are purple.
     Now start coloring Cindy's clothes and write a story about Cindy's
     birthday party.

Write your story ---

----

c)   Here is a birthday party picture. Choose the colours you like and colour the picture. Write your story about a birthday party.

Write your story here: --

Exercise # 3-Find the secret word and write a sentence with it.

- ouslevram- _____ ....
....
- sluogiour- _____ ....
....
- ecelbranoit- _____ ....
....
- adyiloh- _____ ....
....
- ohodourbghien- _____ ....
....

Exercise # 4-Read out loud the list of words with a short—**i-**. **Word List: win, chin, pig, fish, lid, ship, chick, bib, hill, pig, pin, bill, chip** Write the correct pronunciation of the words using the International Phonetic Alphabet (IPA).

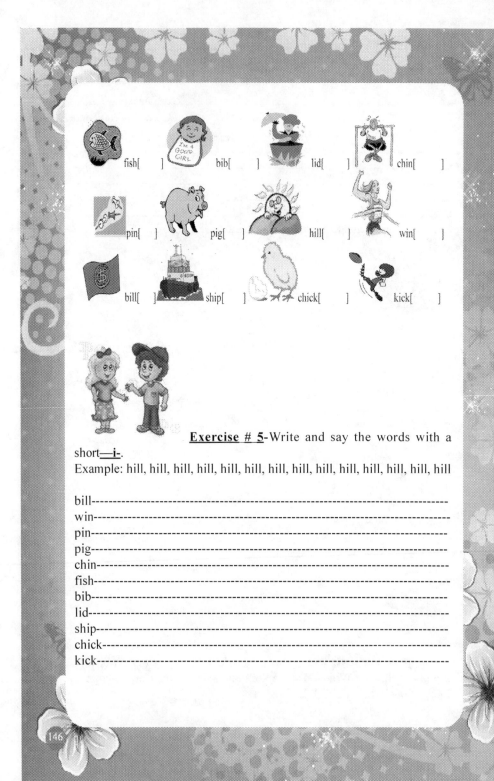

fish[　]　　　bib[　]　　　lid[　]　　　chin[　]

pin[　]　　　pig[　]　　　hill[　]　　　win[　]

bill[　]　　ship[　]　　chick[　]　　kick[　]

Exercise # 5-Write and say the words with a short—**i**-.

Example: hill, hill, hill, hill, hill, hill, hill, hill, hill, hill, hill, hill, hill, hill

bill--
win---
pin---
pig---
chin--
fish--
bib---
lid---
ship--
chick---
kick--

Exercise # 6—Print the word for each picture and pronounce it correctly.

-- -- -- --   -- -- --   -- -- -- --   -- -- --

-- -- -- --   -- -- -- --   -- -- --   -- -- -- -

-- -- -- --   -- -- -- -- --   -- -- -- --   -- -- --

Homework: Write one sentence with each word you learned.

birthday   --

Santa Claus  --

children --

ornaments --

tree --

stocking --

star --

present --

bow --

party --

candles --

balloons ---

SPOT THE MISTAKE—The character in this picture

is a scary character from a Halloween story...........................
....
....
....

REMEMBER THIS-A sentence is a group of words. It tells a complete thought about someone or something. Example: This is a red flower. (This sentence tells something about a flower.)

DID YOU KNOW? Hockey and Lacrosse are the Canadian national sports.

LANGUAGE BANK—In this lesson you learned:

Active words	**Recycled words**	**Passive words**
1. holiday(s)	1. question(s)	1. folks
2. celebration(s)	2. main	2. change
3. celebrate	3. fall	3. movies
4. glorious	4. day(s)	4. sounds
5. notice	5. tree(s)	5. internally
6. marvelous	6. season(s)	6. externally
7. October	7. beautiful	7. divide
8. television	8. special	8. establish

9. typical	9. people	9. incorporate
10. scary	10. right	10. mind
11. neighbourhood	11. blood	11. correlate
12. character(s)	12. eye(s)	12. previously
13. ghost(s)	13. talk about	
14. silly	14. sound	
15. poor	15. think	
16. experience	16. go/went	
17. promise(s)	17. house	
18. the dead	18. popular	
19. pray	19. library	
20. treat(s)	20. children	
21. candy	21. help	
22. thankful	22. connect	
23. decorate	23. a lot of	
24. ornament(s)	24. different	
25. need	25. the same	
26. under	26. sometimes	
27. tie	27. share	
28. bow	28. wavy lines	
29. come	29. some	
30. present(s)	30. painted	
31. ready	31. lemon cake	
32. stocking(s)	32. about	
33. popular		
34. lovely		
35. turned		
36. delicious		
34. lovely		
35. turned		
36. delicious		

Expressions—All Souls Day, trick-and-treat, drop out, in front of, jack-o-lantern, make sure, wake up

Jaguar

Lesson # 9—Travelling
& Short Vowel "E"

Learning goals: A. Learn new words
B. Learn vocabulary about travelling
C. Learn short vowel **"e"**

(The topic for today's class is **travelling**. All the students have had the chance to take a long **trip** to come to their new country. However, it must have been very **difficult** to leave their old country. Today students will share their travelling experiences.)

Mr. Knowitall: Good morning. I **am sorry** I am late for class but **driving** was very difficult this morning. There was a winter **storm** last night and the **roads** were very **slippery** in the morning. Driving to school today was very difficult.

Ben: How do you **usually** come to school, Mr. Knowitall, by **bus** or by car?

Mr. Knowitall: Usually, I take the **train** to school but today I **drove** my car because I have a doctor's **appointment** after school.

Stephen: I **ride** my **bicycle** to school every day. However, today it was very cold and I took the bus.

Paolo: When we left my country to come here, we travelled by **plane**. It was my first time in an airplane and I was very **nervous**.

Karol: I like to travel in summer. **During last** summer **vacation**, my **parents** and I travelled to different **places**.

Ming: I like traveling, too. Last summer, we went to British Columbia by plane. We **visited** my **aunt** who lives in Vancouver. We **took** a **ferry** to go to visit Victoria.

Monique: My grandmother lives in Victoria, too. **Usually**, we take the bus to go from the ferry to my grandmother's house. Now that my father has a car, he drives us to the ferry and then from the ferry to her house. This is much **faster** than taking the bus at the ferry terminal.

Ming: Travelling is so much fun. From the car I can see **trucks** and trains **passing** by. When the weather is good, I like to ride my bicycle around my grandmother's house and feel the wind on my face.

George: (changes the topic) Mr. Knowitall, **yesterday** I **came across** a new English word, "**homophones**". The book, also, said that it is very important to know the different **meanings** of homonyms. Can you **explain** to us what homonyms are?

Mr. Knowitall: You are **making a very good point**, George. It is very important for an English Language Learner (ELL) to know what homonyms are. They are words that may sound **alike** but have different meanings and different **spelling**, like: here-hear, blew-blue, right—write.

Ben: Thank you for explaining that to us, it is a very important piece of information. However, I wanted to ask a question about another concept that is new to me, too. I am talking about something called "**synonyms**". I heard the word in our English Language Arts class but I was uncomfortable to ask the question there.

Mr. Knowitall: That is **another** very good question, Ben. Synonyms are words that have the same or **almost** the same meaning, like: big—large, small—little, happy—jolly.

Karol: Mr. Knowitall, I have read about another word—**antonyms**—that I do not understand. Can you explain to us what antonyms are, please?

Mr. Knowitall: That is a very good question, Karol. You really **need** to know what antonyms are. Antonyms are words that are **opposite** or almost opposite in meaning, like: black-white, short—tall, short—long, day—night.

George: These are very important **concepts** for me as a learner of English. So, (speaks while thinking, reviewing the new information, and speaking very slowly) homonyms sound the same but are different in spelling and meaning; synonyms look different but have almost the same meaning; antonyms have opposite meaning. Now I understand.

Monique: Now I understand the meaning of the words "synonym", "antonym", and "homonym", too, but I would like to **practice** them a little more.

Paolo: Me, too.

Mr. Knowitall: I <u>totally</u> <u>agree</u> with you. We will do some <u>**exercises**</u> that will help you understand those concepts better. We will, also, practice some more English sounds and letters. Let us start.

<u>Practice your knowledge</u>

<u>**Exercise # 1**</u>—Vocabulary study

Task 1—Check the meaning of the following words in your dictionary. Copy the definitions. e. x. <u>**"trip"**</u>—a journey of relatively short duration, especially to a place and back again. Paolo took a trip to the new soccer field.

Task 2—Find the sentence with the same word from the text and copy it or write your own sentence. Follow the example with the word "trip".

❑   **travelling**
Definition ....
Sentence..
❑   **difficult**
Definition ....
Sentence..
❑   **driving**
Definition ....
Sentence..

❑　　**storm(s)**

Definition ....

Sentence ....

❑　　**road(s)**

Definition ....

Sentence ....

❑　　**slippery**

Definition ....

Sentence ....

❑　　**usually**

Definition ....

Sentence ....

❑　　**bus**

Definition ....

Sentence ....

❑　　**train(s)**

Definition ....

Sentence ....

❑　　**drive-drop**

Definition ....

Sentence ....

❑　　**appointment**

Definition ....

Sentence ....

❑　　**ride**

Definition ....

Sentence ....

❑　　**bicycle(s)**

Definition ....

Sentence ....

❑　　**plane(s)**

Definition ....

Sentence ....

❑　　**nervous**

Definition ....

Sentence ....

❑　　**during**

Definition ....

Sentence ....

❑   **vacation(s)**

Definition ....

Sentence..

❑   **place(s)**

Definition ....

Sentence..

❑   **last**

Definition ....

Sentence..

❑   **visit**

Definition ....

Sentence..

❑   **aunt**

Definition ....

Sentence..

❑   **ferry**

Definition ....

Sentence..

❑   **take-took**

Definition ....

Sentence..

❑   **faster**

Definition ....

Sentence..

❑   **truck(s)**

Definition ....

Sentence..

❑   **passing**

Definition ....

Sentence..

❑   **yesterday**

Definition ....

Sentence..

❑   **homophone(s)**

Definition ....

Sentence..

❑   **synonym(s)**

Definition ....

Sentence..

❑   **antonym(s)**
Definition ....
Sentence..
❑   **meaning(s)**
Definition ....
Sentence..
❑   **explain**
Definition ....
Sentence..
❑   **alike**
Definition ....
Sentence..
❑   **spelling**
Definition ....
Sentence..
❑   **another**
Definition ....
Sentence..
❑   **almost**
Definition ....
Sentence..
❑   **need**
Definition ....
Sentence..
❑   **opposite**
Definition ....
Sentence..
❑   **concept(s)**
Definition ....
Sentence..
❑   **practice**
Definition ....
Sentence..
❑   **totally**
Definition ....
Sentence..
❑   **agree**
Definition ....
Sentence..

Definition ....

Sentence...

Exercise # 2—Let us learn the words that are pronounced with a short **"e"**—Word List: **red, bed, ten, men, bell, sell, shell, pet, nest, wet, net** Write the correct pronunciation of the following words by using International Phonetic Alphabet (IPA).

A.   Read the list of words out loud.

bed[ ]   ten[ ]   men[ ]   bell[   ]

shell[ ]   pet[ ]   nest[   ]   wet[   ]

net[ ]   elephant[   ]   entrance[   ]

B.   Write and say the words. Example: net, net, net, net, net, net, net, net, net, net, net, net,

wet---

nest---

bell---

shell---

pet---

bed---

ten---

men---

elephant--
entrance--
envelope--

C. Print and the word for each picture.

-- -- -- --   -- -- --   -- -- --   -- -- --

-- -- -- --   -- -- -- --   -- -- -- -- -- --   -- -- -- -- --

-- -- --   -- -- --   -- -- --   -- -- -- -- -- -- --

Exercise # 3-Unscramble the following groups of letters and find the secret words. Write a sentence with each word. For example: usb—"bus"—I go to school by bus everyday.

- unat-.......................--

- ainrt-.......................--

- yrref-.......................--

- eapln-.....................---

- arc-.....................---

- lcebiyc.....................---

- levart-.....................---

- deir-.....................---

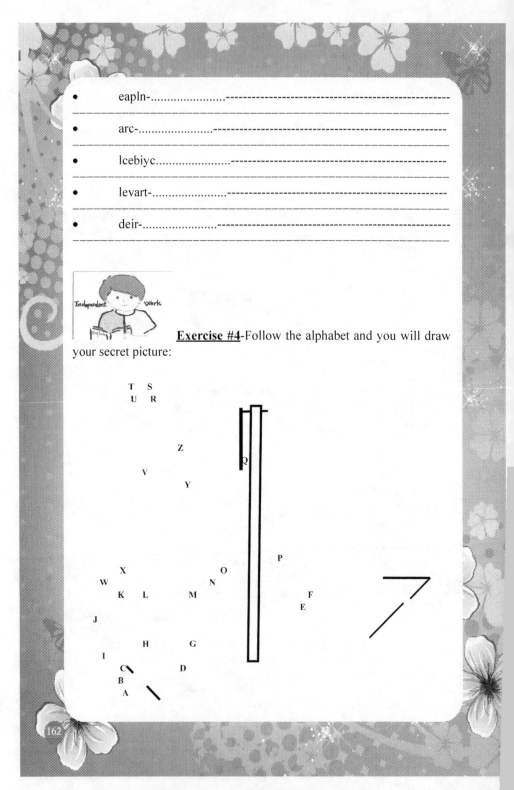

Exercise #4-Follow the alphabet and you will draw your secret picture:

Exercise # 5-Find the words for the following pictures. Copy the sentences with the word from the lesson or write a new sentence with each word.

For example—<u>Picture</u>:  <u>Word</u>: ferry <u>Sentence</u>—We took a ferry to go visit Victoria.

* ....---
----

* ....---
----

* ....---
----

* ....---

- ...._____

- ...._____

- ...._____

- ...._____

- ...._____

- ...._____

Exercise # 6-Work with a friend—Find a synonym from the list of words below for the underlined word in each sentence. Write each sentence using the synonym from the list in place of the underlined word. Use the dictionary if needed.

List of synonyms: guarded, story, woods, still, close, injure, house.

❏   The police searched for the lost boy in the <u>forest.</u>

_____

❏   Please, remember <u>to shut</u> the door closely.

_____

❏   Mom told us <u>the tale</u> of "Cinderella".

_____

❏   They moved into their new <u>home</u> last week.

_____

❏   The dog may <u>hurt</u> the little baby.

_____

❏   Everyone was <u>quiet</u> as they listened for the bell.

_____

❏   The fire fighters <u>protected</u> the building.

_____

Exercise # 7-Let us learn some antonyms, check their meaning in your dictionary. Write the correct word from Column II beside its antonym in Column I.

I		II	I		II	I		II
strong	_____	light	light	_____	tight	large	_____	fearful
dry	_____	few	loose	_____	warm	sharp	_____	spend
hot	_____	wet	cold	_____	dull	sick	_____	dull
dark	_____	weak	fat	_____	heavy	fearless	_____	healthy
many	_____	cold	bright	_____	thin	save	_____	small

I	II	I	II	I	II
asleep _____	fast	swiftly _____	quiet	hard _____	under
slow _____	awake	noisy _____	difficult	young _____	soft
friend _____	sad	easy _____	go	win _____	descend
full _____	enemy	build _____	slowly	over _____	old
happy _____	empty	come _____	destroy	climb _____	lose

Exercise # 8-Let us practice using the correct homophones in the following sentences. Draw a circle around the word that correctly completes each sentence. Then write the complete sentence on the line provided. Look at the example: We asked the (maid , made) to wash the windows. <u>We asked the maid to wash the windows.</u>

❑ The wind (blew, blue) the clouds away. _____
❑ Eric (cent, sent) his puzzle to a friend. _____
❑ We are learning to (right, write) English. _____
❑ Mother was very (weak, week) after being sick. _____
❑ Cindy (through, threw) the ball and broke the window. _____
❑ We (ate, eight) our supper early. _____
❑ The doctor will (be, bee) here in a minute. _____
❑ He went to the shop to (by, buy) a new software. _____
❑ The lady gave the driver her bus (fare, fair). _____
❑ The new Disney movie lasted an (our, hour). _____
❑ She (red, read) a new book this week. _____

Homework: You can travel by bus, train, car, or ship. Describe one kind of trip you liked best and tell us why you like it so much. Use new words you learned in the lesson.

....
....

....
....
....
....
....
....
....
....
....
....
....
....

SPOT THE MISTAKE—My ride to school is very short

because I ride this bus   every day. There are some mistakes in this sentence. Find them.

1. --
2. --
3. --
4. --

STUDY TIP—Many students struggle with school academic reading. The reason for this is because they have limited academic vocabulary. So, if you want to improve your reading skills, it is very important that you improve your academic vocabulary.

REMEMBER THIS-We say "Bon Voyage" when people leave for a trip by plane, ship, train, or bus.

DID YOU KNOW? Two words that share the same meaning are called synonyms.

LANGUAGE BANK—In this lesson you learned:

Active words	Recycled words	Passive words
1. travelling	1. student	1. topic
2. trip(s)	2. come	2. however
3. difficult	3. country	3. but
4. driving	4. leave-left	4. when
5. storm(s)	5. old	5. after
6. road(s)	6. experience(s)	6. definition(s)
7. slippery	7. share	7. pair(s)
8. usually	8. must	8. sound
9. bus	9. morning	9. each other
10. train(s)	10. winter	10. confused
11. drive-drop	11. night	11. easily
12. appointment(s)	12. car	12. be careful
13. ride	13. cold	13. correct
14. bicycle(s)	14. like	14 express something

15. plane(s)
16. nervous
17. during
18. vacation(s)
19. place(s)
20. last
21. visit
22. ferry
23. take/took
24. faster
25. truck(s)
26. passing
27. conductor
28. homophones(s)
29. synonym(s)
30. antonym(s)
31. meaning(s)
32. explain
33. alike
34. spelling
35. another
36. almost
37. need
38. opposite
39. concept(s)
40. practice
41. totally
42. agree
43. exercisc(s)

15. summer
16. different
17. go-went
18. live
19. grandmother
20. too
21. house
22. important
23. something

Expressions: have the chance, I am sorry, come across, make a point

15. meaning
16. entrance
17. envelope
18. elephant
19. first time
20. really
21. forest/woods
22. shut/close
23. tale/story
24. hurt/injure
25. quiet/still
26. protect/guard
27. wet/dry
28. light/dark
29. light/heavy
30. strong/weak
31. loose/tight
32. lose/win
33. spend/save
34. sharp/dull
35. fearless/fearful
36. fat/thin
37. bright/dull
38. friend/enemy
39. asleep/awake
40. full/empty
41. hard/soft
42. quiet/noisy
43. over/under
44. climb/descend

Lesson 10—My Body, My Health & Short "a+r"

(Mr.Knowitall is very happy with the way his students are **improving** their English **proficiency** and **especially** their correct **pronunciation** and **spelling**. He knows that they are **working hard** to learn more English words and expressions and to **communicate** better. Today he is planning to talk about situations **connected** with the human body and **health.**)

Mr. Knowitall: Good morning everybody. My son, Nick, came home for the holidays yesterday and we are so glad to have him home for two weeks.

Karol: Why, doesn't he live with you all the time, Mr. Knowitall?

Mr. Knowitall: No, he goes to university in another town. He is studying **medicine** because he wants to become a **cardiologist.**

George: Does it take long for him to come home from the other town, Mr. Knowitall?

Mr. Knowitall: No, not really. He drives his car for about two hours. However, this time his trip took three hours because the roads were slippery and there were many **accidents** on the roads.

Monique: (thinking and speaking with a low voice) I would like to **become** a doctor someday, too.

Paolo: Why not, Monique. I would be your first **patient** (laughs).

Ben: (being funny) In fact, I will be your first patient, **right now.** Do you know anything about feet? My feet and **toes** get **itchy, peely** and dry all the time.

Monique: I am not a doctor but it sounds like this may be a **sign** that you have athlete's feet. This situation is not difficult and can be easily **treated**. What other signs do you have, Ben?

Ben: Usually, I have **blisters**, **cracked skin**, dry and red feet, especially between my toes. Let me show you in a drawing how my feet look. (draws on a piece of paper) Here is my drawing for you:

Signs of
Athlete's Feet
Blisters
Cracked skin
Rash
Dry and
red feet
Itching

Monique: I see your situation, Ben. It is **important** not **to scratch** your feet, because the **infection** can **spread** and it will not make the problem any better.

Ben: You already sound like a doctor, Monique. Thanks for your advice.

Stephen: I want **to share** a situation with you Monique, too. My parents are very unhappy because my brother has started **smoking** and that is a very **bad habit**.

Paolo: Your brother may be under **peer pressure**, Stephen. While we are **growing up**, we may **face** peer pressure to take **drugs** or smoke. The **decisions** we make in these situations are up to us. We are the only ones who can **make healthy choices** for our **mind** and body.

George: When people smoke, they are using something called **tobacco**. Tobacco **contains** a **substance** called nicotine, which is very **addictive,** meaning it is difficult to stop putting nicotine into your body after you've started smoking.

Mr. Knowitall: You are right, George. **Cigarette** smoking is usually a form of using tobacco. Cigarettes and cigars are especially bad for us because tobacco smoke puts many **poisons** into our **mouth**, **throat**, and **lungs**. It, also, **pollutes** the air around the smoker.

George: Smoking, also, **affects our appearance. Exposure** to tobacco smoke can make the teeth and **fingernails** yellow, we will have bad **breath** and bad smell on hair, clothes, and our house. People who smoke die of lung and throat **cancer** or **heart attack**. 400,000 cigarette smokers **die** each year from smoking cigarettes.

Karol: Another difficult situation is when our body is changing all the time and it is hard to **accept** it **all at once**. Body image is important and it means how we see our body. We only get one body and our body is like our home. So, we must love the body we have. There are millions of different bodies in the **world** and each one is very **unique**. Nobody should tell a person how to look or what is acceptable.

Ming: Of course, all bodies are different. There is no perfect body, no matter what we may see on television or in **magazines**. Our body is very special and we need to be comfortable with the way we look. If we eat right and exercise, our body will be what it should be.

Mr. Knowitall: You are right, Ming. Just remember, there is no one **"perfect** body" because we are all different and that difference makes us special. It can be difficult to **keep that in mind** because so many people try to tell us what is attractive, but do not **pay attention** to them.

Monique: One way to feel better about ourselves when people talk about our body is through good **hygiene** skills. Clean hair, showering/bathing and taking care of our skin, teeth and nails can improve our body image and help to keep us healthy.

Mr. Knowitall: Yes, hygiene is very important for our health. In fact, the word ``Hygiene`` comes from the Greek and it means "the art of good health".

Ben: That is very true. **No matter** how much we wish we had green eyes or size 6 feet, it will not happen. It is best just to accept who we are, because we are unique and **fabulous**. It is not our body that is important and makes us who we are. We are not our stomach or arms. We are who we are on the **inside** and that is what is important.

Mr. Knowitall: Appearance is always a big problem for people your **age**. Your body is changing, so things look different sometimes and you may not feel **attractive**. Also, during this time many of you begin to wear glasses or braces. That can make you feel "different" from your friends. Then, of course, there are television and magazine models or "perfect people" that change the way we think of ourselves. However, these are not important. What is important is to know that you are special and unique and there is no body like you in the world.

Practice your knowledge

write on!

Exercise # 1—Vocabulary study.

Task 1—Check the meaning of the following words in your dictionary. Copy the definitions. e. x. **"improve"**—make or become better. Mr. Knowitall helps us improve our English reading skills.

Task 2—Find the sentence with the same word from the text and copy it or write your own sentence. Follow the example with the word "improve".

❑ **proficiency**

Definition ....

Sentence ....

❑ **especially**

Definition ....

Sentence ....

❑ **pronunciation**

Definition ....

Sentence ....

❑ **spelling**

Definition ....

Sentence ....

❑ **communicate**

Definition ....

Sentence ....

❑ **connect**

Definition ....

Sentence ....

❑ **health**

Definition ....

Sentence ....

❑ **medicine**

Definition ....

Sentence ....

❑ **cardiologist**

Definition ....

Sentence ....

❑ **accident(s)**

Definition ....

Sentence ....

❑ **become**

Definition ....

Sentence ....

❑ **patient(s)**

Definition ....

Sentence ....

❑ **toe(s)**

Definition ....

Sentence ....

❑ **itchy**

Definition ....

Sentence ....

❑ **peely**

Definition ....

Sentence ....

❑ **blister(s)**

Definition ....

Sentence ....

❑ **sign(s)**

Definition ....

Sentence ....

❑ **treated**

Definition ....

Sentence ....

❑ **cracked**

Definition ....

Sentence ....

❑ **skin**

Definition ....

Sentence ....

❑ **important**

Definition ....

Sentence ....

❑ **scratch**

Definition ....

Sentence ....

❑ **spread**

Definition ....

Sentence ....

❑ **share**

Definition ....

Sentence ....

❑ **smoking**

Definition ....

Sentence ....

❑ **bad**

Definition ....

Sentence ....

❑ **habit(s)**

Definition ....

Sentence ....

❑　　　**drug(s)**
Definition ....
Sentence ....
❑　　　**decision(s)**
Definition ....
Sentence ....
❑　　　**mind**
Definition ....
Sentence ....
❑　　　**tobacco**
Definition ....
Sentence ....
❑　　　**contain**
Definition ....
Sentence ....
❑　　　**substance(s)**
Definition ....
Sentence ....
❑　　　**addictive**
Definition ....
Sentence ....
❑　　　**cigarette(s)**
Definition ....
Sentence ....
❑　　　**cigar(s)**
Definition ....
Sentence ....
❑　　　**poison(s)**
Definition ....
Sentence ....
❑　　　**mouth(s)**
Definition ....
Sentence ....
❑　　　**throat(s)**
Definition ....
Sentence ....
❑　　　**lung(s)**
Definition ....
Sentence ....

❑ **pollute**

Definition ....

Sentence ....

❑ **breath**

Definition ....

Sentence ....

❑ **affect**

Definition ....

Sentence ....

❑ **appearance(s)**

Definition ....

Sentence ....

❑ **exposure(s)**

Definition ....

Sentence ....

❑ **fingernail(s)**

Definition ....

Sentence ....

❑ **accept**

Definition ....

Sentence ....

❑ **million(s)**

Definition ....

Sentence ....

❑ **world**

Definition ....

Sentence ....

❑ **unique**

Definition ....

Sentence ....

❑ **magazine(s)**

Definition ....

Sentence ....

❑ **fabulous**

Definition ....

Sentence ....

❑ **inside**

Definition ....

Sentence ....

❑   **age**

Definition ....

Sentence..

❑   **attractive**

Definition ....

Sentence..

❑   **brace(s)**

Definition ....

Sentence..

Exercise # 2-Some words end in ``ar`` and some other words have ``ar`` in the middle and their pronunciation may be different. Let us learn the correct pronunciation of those words.

Word List: car, far, star, park, shark, start, party, jar, scar, art, dark, garden, tart

A.   Read these words out loud and write them in the space provided.

car   star   jar   park

shark   party   garden   tart

Example: car, car, car, car, car, car, car, car, car, car, car, car, car, car, car, car, car, car, car,

far_____

star_____

park_____
shark_____
start_____
party_____
jar_____
scar_____
art_____
dark_____
tart_____
garden_____

Exercise # 3-Find the secret word and write a sentence with it.

- ecnyicifpro......................._____
  _____

- diooltsigdrac......................._____
  _____

- dadictevi......................._____
  _____

- ersblits......................._____
  _____

- ttraoh................_____
  _____

Exercise # 4-Complete the ``ar``words with one of these letters c, p, k, j, g, d, e, n, h, s, t, y, and draw a line to connect the word with the correct object.

___ ___ a r

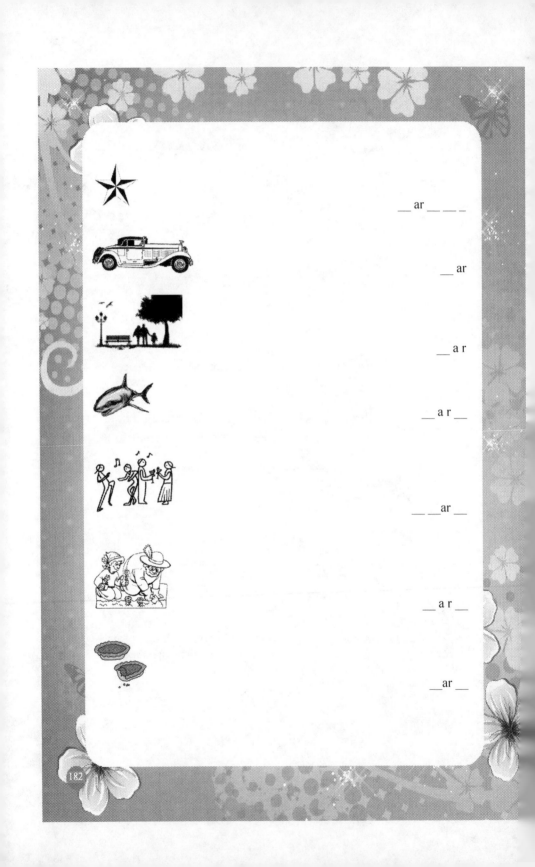

__ ar __ __ _

__ ar

__ a r

__ a r __

__ __ ar __

__ a r __

__ ar __

182

Exercise # 5-Find the words, draw pictures of the objects and complete the sentences.

- sh __ __ k   _____ has sharp teeth.
- m __ __ ket   My mother buys vegetables in the _____.
- p __ __ k   I ride my bicycle in the _____.

Homework: Choose ten new words from Exercise # 1 and write one sentence with each word you choose. Remember to underline the new word you are using.

1. ....
....
2. ....
....
3. ....
....
4. ....
....
5. ....
....
6. ....
....
7. ....
....
8. ....
....
9. ....
....
10. ....
....

STUDY TIP—Learning the correct pronunciation of English words is a very important part of your studies. It does not matter so much if you just want to read and/or write the language, but if you want to speak a language well, you must pay special attention to the correct pronunciation and review it regularly.

SPOT THE MISTAKE—These fingernails are very clean and healthy.

Signs of
Athlete's Feet!
Blisters
Cracked skin
Rash
Dry and
red feet
Itching

....
....
....
....

REMEMBER THIS-A homograph is a word that has the same spelling as another word. Homographs have the same spelling but they differ from each other in meaning, origin, and sometimes pronunciation. E. x. wave—greet somebody by moving your hand, waves of the sea

DID YOU KNOW? The longest street in the world is Yonge Street in the Province of Ontario, Canada. Yonge Street starts at Lake Ontario and runs north through central and northern Ontario to the Ontario—Minnesota border. It is over 1178 miles or 1896 kilometers. The Guinness Book of World Records recognized this special street in 1998.

LANGUAGE BANK—In this lesson you learned:

Active words	**Recycled words**	**Passive words**
1. proficiency	1. happy	1. between
2. especially	2. student(s)	2. only
3. pronunciation	3. know	3. using
4. spelling	4. remember	4. when
5. communicate	5. expression(s)	5. just
6. connect	6. word(s)	6. through
7. health	7. today	7. healthy
8. medicine	8. body	8. true
9. cardiologist	9. home(s)	9. always
10. accident(s)	10. come	
11. become	11. drive	
12. patient(s)	12. trip(s)	
13. toe(s)	13. road(s)	
14. itchy	14. slippery	
15. peely	15. doctor(s)	
16. blister(s)	16. dry	
17. sign(s)	17. usually	
18. treated	18. situation(s)	
19. cracked	19. sound(s)	
20. skin	20. difficult	

21. important
22. scratch
23. spread
24. share
25. smoking
26. bad
27. habit(s)
28. drug(s)
29. decision(s)
30. mind
31. tobacco
32. contain
33. substance(s)
34. addictive
35. cigarette(s)
36. cigar(s)
37. poison(s)
38. mouth(s)
39. throat(s)
40. lung(s)
41. pollute
42. breath
43. affect
44. appearance(s)
45. exposure(s)
46. fingernail(s)
47. accept
48. million(s)
49. world
50. unique
51. magazine(s)

21. easily
22. show
23. drawing
24. something
25. called
26. smell

Expressions: work hard, right now, grow up, pay attention, no matter, peer pressure, make healthy choices, heart attack, all at once, keep in mind

52. fabulous
53. inside
54. age
55. attractive
56. brace(s)

L Lamb
leaf

Lesson 11—Emotional Health & Hard and Soft "C"

Learning goals: A. Learn about emotional health
B. Learn new words about health
C. Learn how to say words with **"C"**

(Mr. Knowitall **enjoyed** the discussion about the healthy choices yesterday. He thinks that his students may enjoy a discussion about their **emotional health,** too. He **believes** that will be a very important discussion for his students.)

Mr. Knowitall: Good morning folks. I enjoyed our talk yesterday about healthy choices. Your comments were very good. I want to **continue** our discussion on the **same** **topic** but today we will **focus** on our emotional health. What do you think of this idea?

Ben: I don't believe we have discussed about emotional health before, Mr. Knowitall. What is good emotional health?

Mr. Knowitall: Yes, Ben, this is the first time we are talking about emotional health and I believe it is very important to know more about it. People who have good emotional health **are aware** of their thoughts, **feelings** and **behaviors**. They learn healthy ways to **cope with stress** and problems that are a part of our daily life. They feel good about themselves and have healthy **relationships**.

Stephen: I **am interested in** learning about emotional health because many things that **happen** in our life can **disrupt** our studies and lead to strong feelings of **sadness**, stress, or **anxiety**. What are the **main characteristics** of emotional health, Mr. Knowitall?

Paolo: I have taken a class about emotional health and I can answer some of your questions, Stephen. The main characteristics of emotional health include situations when people who **lose their job**, have a child who is very sick, **deal** with the **death** of a loved one, **get divorced**, **get married** or have a baby, and, especially, when people **move to** a new country.

Karol: It sounds like even "good" **changes** can be just as stressful as "bad" changes and in fact those strong emotions **affect** our health.

Ming: Our body **responds** to the way we think, feel and act. This is called the "mind/body **connection**." When we are stressed, anxious or **upset**, our body tries to tell us that something isn't right. For example, **high blood pressure** or other **diseases** may **develop** after stressful situations, such as the death of a loved one.

Mr. Knowitall: Poor emotional health can have the following physical signs: back **pain**, change in **appetite**, chest pain, **headaches**, high blood pressure, and people may **gain** or **lose weight**. Also, when you are feeling stressed, anxious or upset, you may not take care of your health as well as you should. You may not feel like **exercising**, eating healthy foods or taking walks. Some people may take **alcohol**, tobacco or other drugs when they have poor emotional health.

Monique—So, how can I **improve** my emotional health, Mr. Knowitall?

Ming: I asked my doctor the same question and this is what he said—First, try to **recognize** your emotions and understand why you are having them. Finding the **causes** of sadness, stress and anxiety in your life can help you improve your emotional health.

Mr. Knowitall: Also, there are different ways to improve our emotional stress. I have put some notes on each of your desks; please, share them with our class.

George: (reads) **Share your feelings.** If feelings of stress, sadness or anxiety are causing physical or emotional problems, keeping these feelings **inside** can make you feel worse. It's OK to let your loved ones know when something is **bothering** you. However, **keep in mind** that your family and friends may not be able to help you deal with your feelings. At these times, ask someone **outside** the situation—such as your family doctor, a **counselor**, or a teacher to help you improve your emotional health.

Ben: (reads) Live a **balanced** life. Try not to think about the problems at work, school or home that lead to bad feelings. This doesn't mean you have to be happy when you feel stressed, anxious or upset. It is important to deal with these negative feelings, but try to focus on the good things in your life, too. You may want to write a **journal** about things that make you feel happy. Having good feelings can improve your life and give you a good emotional health. **Make time** for things you **enjoy**.

Karol: (reads) Develop **resilience**. People with resilience are able to cope with stress in a healthy way. Resilience can be learned in different ways. These include having **social** support, keeping a good behaviour, **accepting** change and building hope.

Stephen: (reads) **Calm** your mind and body. **Relaxation** methods are good ways to bring your emotions into balance. **Meditation** is a form of **thinking**. It can take many forms. For example, you may do it by exercising or listening to music. Ask your family doctor to learn more about relaxation methods.

Paolo: (reads) Take care of yourself. To have good emotional health, it is important to take care of your body by having **regular** times for eating healthy meals, getting enough good **sleep** and exercising. Do not smoke or take drugs and alcohol. Using drugs or alcohol just causes other problems, such as family and health problems.

Mr. Knowitall: So, we need to take good care of our emotional health because it will help our physical health, too. Our mind and our body work together to give us a healthy life and we need to take good care of both the mind and the body. This is the end of our class for today. I hope you enjoyed the discussion. Let us work with some exercises now.

Practice your knowledge

Exercise # 1—Vocabulary study.

Task 1—Check the meaning of the following words in your dictionary. Copy the definitions. e. x. **"enjoy"**—to like something very much. Mr. Knowitall's students enjoyed their discussion about the emotional health.

Task 2—Find the sentence with the same word from the text and copy it or write your own sentence. Follow the example with the word "enjoy".

❑ **believe**
Definition ....
Sentence..

❏ **feeling(s)**

Definition ....

Sentence ....

❏ **continue**

Definition ....

Sentence ....

❏ **same**

Definition ....

Sentence ....

❏ **topic(s)**

Definition ....

Sentence ....

❏ **behaviour**

Definition ....

Sentence ....

❏ **stress**

Definition ....

Sentence ....

❏ **relationship(s)**

Definition ....

Sentence ....

❏ **happen**

Definition ....

Sentence ....

❏ **disrupt**

Definition ....

Sentence ....

❏ **sadness**

Definition ....

Sentence ....

❏ **anxiety**

Definition ....

Sentence ....

❏ **main**

Definition ....

Sentence ....

❏ **characteristic(s)**

Definition ....

Sentence ....

❑ **deal with**

Definition ....

Sentence ....

❑ **death**

Definition ....

Sentence ....

❑ **move to**

Definition ....

Sentence ....

❑ **change(s)**

Definition ....

Sentence ....

❑ **stressful**

Definition ....

Sentence ....

❑ **affect**

Definition ....

Sentence ....

❑ **respond**

Definition ....

Sentence ....

❑ **connection(s)**

Definition ....

Sentence ....

❑ **upset**

Definition ....

Sentence ....

❑ **disease(s)**

Definition ....

Sentence ....

❑ **develop**

Definition ....

Sentence ....

❑ **pain(s)**

Definition ....

Sentence ....

❑ **appetite**

Definition ....

Sentence ....

❏　　headache

Definition ....

Sentence ....

❏　　gain

Definition ....

Sentence ....

❏　　weight

Definition ....

Sentence ....

❏　　lose

Definition ....

Sentence ....

❏　　exercising

Definition ....

Sentence ....

❏　　alcohol

Definition ....

Sentence ....

❏　　improve

Definition ....

Sentence ....

❏　　recognize

Definition ....

Sentence ....

❏　　cause(s)

Definition ....

Sentence ....

❏　　inside

Definition ....

Sentence ....

❏　　outside

Definition ....

Sentence ....

❏　　bothering

Definition ....

Sentence ....

❏　　counselor(s)

Definition ....

Sentence ....

❑　　**balanced**
Definition ....
Sentence..
❑　　**journal(s)**
Definition ....
Sentence..
❑　　**resilience**
Definition ....
Sentence..
❑　　**social**
Definition ....
Sentence..
❑　　**support**
Definition ....
Sentence..
❑　　**accept**
Definition ....
Sentence..
❑　　**calm**
Definition ....
Sentence..
❑　　**relaxation**
Definition ....
Sentence..
❑　　**meditation**
Definition ....
Sentence..
❑　　**regular**
Definition ....
Sentence..
❑　　**sleep**
Definition ....
Sentence..

Exercise #2:-Read the following story and learn the new words. Write your own "picture story" about emotions.

I have a little brother . Sometimes he is happy

and sometimes he is sad . When he is tired he rubs his

ear and yawns then he falls asleep . If dad

does not talk to him, he is sad and sometimes gets

angry . One day, my brother and I were playing in

the garden . A big, black dog came to our garden.

My brother was scared and started crying . However,

the dog was very nice. My brother was surprised  and started

laughing . This made me very happy .

❖ Here are pictures for some of the words and emotions from the story:

emotions , brother , happy , sad

, rub the ear , to yawn , fall asleep , dad

, to talk , angry , playing , garden

, scared , crying , surprised ,

laughing , happy .

❖ **Now write your picture story about emotions:** ....
....
....
....
....
....

....
....
....
....
....

Exercise # 3-Find the secret word and write a sentence with it.

❖ alrexniaot _____ -------------------------------------

❖ ecreienlis _____ -------------------------------------

❖ ringbohter _____ -------------------------

❖ ezgniocre _____ ----------------------

Exercise # 4-Pronunciation of the words with the letter "C" in them can be a problem. Sometimes the "C" can be soft and sometimes it can be hard. Let us learn how to pronounce hard and soft "C" words.

❖ Read this list of words out loud.

grocery	doctor	candy	recess	cement
decide	cookies	price	cattle	corn
force	decorate	crib	cow	grace
actor	cellar	palace	carriage	cemetery

❖   Divide the words from the above list into two groups. Under the cake write the words that contain a hard "C", under the pencil write the words that contain a soft "C".

When "C" is followed by "e", "i", or "y", the "C" is usually soft. Soft "C" sounds like the sound "S".

When "C" is followed by "a", "o" or "u", the "C" sound is usually hard. Hard "C" sounds like the sound "K".

_____   _____

_____   _____

_____   _____

_____   _____

_____   _____

_____   _____

_____   _____

_____   _____

_____

Exercise # 5-Let us practice the new rules we learned. Mickey the Mouse is looking at the pieces of cheese. He needs to find the correct pronunciation of each word with "C" sound but he is not sure. He must colour the words with the hard **"C"** in yellow and the words with soft **"C"** in orange. Can you help him?

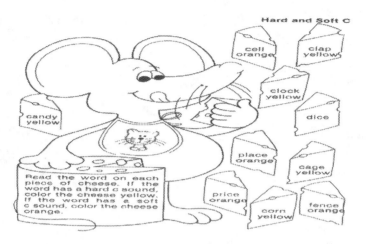

❖ The girl needs to colour the balls in yellow and orange: yellow for hard **"C"** sounds and orange for soft **"C"** sounds. Work with a friend and colour the balls.

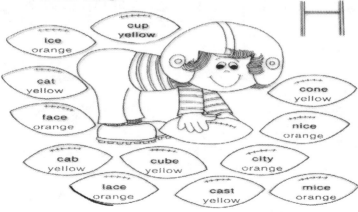

STUDY TIP—Building up your vocabulary in the English language can take many years. Learning words in context from written and spoken material is the most effective way to do this. You can, also, try learning words in a more systematic way—perhaps a certain number (20-25 words) of words every day.

SPOT THE MISTAKE—This girl is happy and is especially funny.

....
....
....
....

REMEMBER THIS-If you keep writing in your journal every day, you will have many ideas how to write well.

DID YOU KNOW? The Trans-Canada Highway between Victoria, British Columbia and St. John's, Newfoundland, in Canada is the world's longest national highway with a length of 7,821 km or 4,860 miles.

LANGUAGE BANK—In this lesson you learned:

Active words	**Recycled words**	**Passive words**
1. believe	1. discussion(s)	1. highway
2. feeling(s)	2. healthy	2. keep writing
3. continue	3. choice(s)	3. world
4. same	4. yesterday	4. national
5. topic(s)	5. today	5. length
6. behaviour	6. think	6, mile(s)
7. stress	7. important	7. idea(s)
8. relationship(s)	8. comment(s)	8. building
9. happen	9. situation(s)	9. vocabulary
10. disrupt	10. child	10. learning
11. sadness	11. sick	11. context
12. anxiety	12. medicine	12. material
13. main	13. especially	13. effective
14. characteristic(s)	14. sound	14. certain
15. deal with	15. strong	15. try
16. death	16. tobacco	16. systematic
17. move to	17. drug(s)	17. spoken
18. change(s)	18. take care of	18. hard
19. stressful	19. take	19. soft
20. affect	20. find	20. strip

21. respond
22. connection(s)
23. upset
24. disease(s)
25. develop
26. pain(s)
27. appetite
28. headache
29. gain
30. weight

31. lose
32. exercising
33. alcohol
34. recognize
35. cause(s)
36. inside
37. outside
38. bothering
39. counselor(s)
40. balanced
41. journal(s)
42. sleep
43. resilience
44. social
45. support
46. accept
47. calm
48. relaxation
49. meditation
50. regular

21. share
22. someone
23. happy
24. focus
25. improve
26. number
27. research

Expressions: emotional health, be aware of, cope with stress, be interested in . . . , lose the job, lose weight, get married, get divorced, high blood pressure, keep in mind, make time for . . . .

21. decide
22. cut
23. paste

Mm

MITTENS

Lesson 12—Shopping for Clothes & Hard and Soft "G"

Learning goals: A. Learn how to communicate
B. Improve English vocabulary
C. Learn the pronunciation of <u>**"G"**</u>

(Mr. Knowitall knows that students are very <u>**interested**</u> in <u>**shopping**</u>, so he has chosen to close this book with a discussion about shopping. The main objective: Students will be able to request information in a <u>**department store**</u>).

Mr. Knowitall: Good morning, everyone. The weather these days has been very good. This is the best weather for going shopping. Do you like going shopping?

Karol: I like to go shopping. Sometimes I buy things and sometimes I just enjoy <u>**window shopping**</u>.

Ben: I totally **hate** shopping but last week I had to go shopping with my parents because we needed some ornaments for our Christmas tree. It was a stressful **experience**; it wasted my time but I had no choice because my parents do not speak English and I had to go with them.

Monique: I can't understand you, Ben. Usually, people enjoy going shopping. You **develop** relationships with people, learn new words, practice your English and buy things you need for you and your family.

Ben: Yes, Monique, I can see your point but usually men don't like shopping. However, I agree with you, shopping can help us practice English.

Mr. Knowitall: That is **exactly** what I have planned for today: We are going to role-play different **situations** **related** to shopping. All of us will **participate** in different **dialogues** and then we will go to the **shopping mall.**. Let us start with the first dialogue, Ming, Stephen and Paolo will you play the main characters, please.

DIALOG NUMBER 1 IN THE SHOPPING MALL:

Stephen: **Excuse me**, where are the **dress shoes**?

Paolo: They're **over there** in the shoe department.

 Stephen: Do you have the kind of shoes without **laces**?

 Paolo: Sure. They're over there on your right.

 Ming: (talking to Stephen) What **size** shoe do you **wear**?

 Stephen: I wear size nine and a **half**.

 Ming: (gives a pair of shoes to Stephen) Here, try these on.

 Stephen: (tries the shoes on) They are a little **too big**.

 Ming: (gives another pair) **How about** these?

Stephen: (tries the shoes on) They are just **right**. **How much** are they?

Ming: They're $19.95. They're **on sale** this week.

Stephen: Good, I'll take them.

Mr. Knowitall: That was a great dialogue, thank you. Did you learn anything new?

Ming: I learned many new words and how to ask questions. It was very **helpful.**

Mr. Knowitall: Ok. Let us do another **dialogue**. This time the characters will be Carol and Monique.

George: Mr. Knowitall, I have **checked** the **dictionary** and I have made a **list** of other words that we may **need** to know when we go shopping. That list would help us to **expand** our **vocabulary**. Can I share some more words with my **peers**?

Mr. Knowitall: Of course, George. Go ahead.

George: Here they are: Excuse me, where are the tennis shoes? . . . . woman's dresses? . . . . boy's pants? . . . . towels? . . . . sheets? Do you have shoes without laces? . . . . with **buckles**? . . . . with **high heels**?

Ben: In order to answer George's questions we need more words and expressions. I have a list of some more words we can use when shopping. May I **add** some more, Mr. Knowitall?

Mr. Knowitall: (very proud of his students) Of course, Ben. Please, do.

Ben: For example: They're over there . . . . (point to the place). In the shoe department . . . . in **sportswear** department . . . . in women's wear department . . . . in children's wear department . . . . on **aisle** number 9 . . . . on aisle number 10. They're over there on your right . . . . on your left.

Mr. Knowitall: Thank you, both of you. Those are very important words and expressions. Okay. Now let us listen to Monique and Carol's dialogue.

DIALOGUE # 2—SALES IN SEARS

Karol: (the store **clerk**) Hi. Welcome to *Sears*. Can I help you find something?

Monique: (the client) I'm not sure. Aren't you having a sale right now?

Karol: Everything on these two **racks** over here is on sale.

Monique: Thanks. (very happy) WOW. This **sweater** is nice. But it looks a little too big. Do you have this in a smaller size?

Karol: (**politely** and ready to help) I think so. Let me look. Oh, here's one. Would you like to use the **fitting room** to try it on?

Monique: Sure. Thanks.

Karol: (a little later) How did it **fit**?

Monique: Not too bad. I think I'll take it.

Karol: Great. (She takes it off the **hanger**) How would you like to pay?

Monique: Well, I'm **almost maxed out** on my credit card, so I think I'll pay with a **cheque.**

Karol: Okay, with **tax** it **comes to** $24.93.

Monique: Who should I make the cheque out to?

 Karol: Please, make it out to *Sears*.

 Monique: (hands the cheque to the clerk) Here you are.

 Karol: Can I see some I.D. too, please?

 Monique: Sure, here is my **driver's license**.

 Karol: Thanks. Here you go. Enjoy your sweater. And have a nice day.

 Monique: Thanks. You, too.

Paolo: Mr. Knowitall, Stephen and I have done some research and we have **compiled** a list of expressions about shopping. Can we share our expressions and their **explanations**?

Mr. Knowitall: Please, do.

Stephen: I will go first. In the previous dialogue we heard the clerk say: **are you just looking?** That expression means—do you want to look alone and not buy anything?

Paolo: Another expression we heard was—**to have a sale**—that means that a store will have many things at a **discount price** (*The store is having a sale.*)

Stephen: The girls used another expression-**to be on sale**—that means that one or more **items** are sold at a discount price (*This shirt is on sale.*)

Paolo: We noticed that the store clerk took the sweater off the—**hanger**-. A hanger holds the clothes (shows a picture of a hanger)

Stephen: Another word used in the dialogue was—**rack**—A rack is a metal (or other kind) **bar** that holds clothes. You put your clothes on a hanger and then put the hanger on a rack.

Paolo: Before we decide to buy something, we need to try it on to see that it **fits**. That is when we use the—**fitting room**-. That is a special place in the store where you try on clothes.

Stephen: I hope you noticed an **interesting** expression in the dialogue:—**max out a credit card**-. That is a **slang** expression and it means you have **reached** your **spending limit**. If you cannot spend more money on your credit card, you have maxed it out.

Paolo: Another shopping question is—**how would you like to pay?**—That means "do you want to pay with cash, a credit card, debit card, or a cheque?"

Stephen: After you leave the fitting room, the store clerk may ask: **how does it fit?** She means, "is it a good size for you?"

Paolo: When the client says **"I'll take it"**, it means that she likes it, it is the right size and she wants to buy it.

Stephen: When a person writes a cheque, it is very important to write it to the right person or store. So, the client asks: **who should I make the check out to?**—that means: what name should I write on the cheque?

Paolo: Usually, the store clerk adds extra money to the price and it goes to the government. That is called—**tax-**

Stephen: In order to see that the person who writes the cheque is in fact the same person as the client, the clerk asks for an—**I.D.**—That is an identification (card) and usually it has the person's picture on it.

Mr. Knowitall: (very excited) Wow! That is a very clear explanation of all the expressions we heard in the dialogue. Paolo and Stephen, you **make me very proud** because you did research on all the expressions that we use in shopping. That gives us a clear explanation of what we are learning. In the next book, they are going to be my teaching assistants. (laughs)

So, we come to the end of Book 4 of the Fun English series. You have improved your English proficiency a lot and we will have more fun in Book 5. Thank you for your hard work.

<u>Practice your knowledge</u>

<u>Exercise # 1</u>-Vocabulary study.

Task 1—Check the meaning of the following words in your dictionary. Copy the definitions. e. x. **<u>"dialogue"</u>**—talk between two people. For example: We practice dialogues to improve our English proficiency.

Task 2—Find the sentence with the same word from the text and copy it or write your own sentence. Follow the example with the word "dialogue".

❑　　　**interested**
Definition ....
Sentence..
❑　　　**department store**
Definition ....
Sentence..
❑　　　**hate**
Definition ....
Sentence..
❑　　　**develop**
Definition ....
Sentence..
❑　　　**exactly**
Definition ....
Sentence..
❑　　　**situation(s)**
Definition ....
Sentence..

❑　　　**participate**

Definition ....

Sentence ....

❑　　　**related**

Definition ....

Sentence ....

❑　　　**dress shoes**

Definition ....

Sentence ....

❑　　　**lace(s)**

Definition ....

Sentence ....

❑　　　**wear**

Definition ....

Sentence ....

❑　　　**size(s)**

Definition ....

Sentence ....

❑　　　**half**

Definition ....

Sentence ....

❑　　　**try on**

Definition ....

Sentence ....

❑　　　**too big**

Definition ....

Sentence ....

❑　　　**right(a)**

Definition ....

Sentence ....

❑　　　**right(b)**

Definition ....

Sentence ....

❑　　　**helpful**

Definition ....

Sentence ....

❑　　　**to check**

Definition ....

Sentence ....

❑   **the cheque**

Definition ....

Sentence ....

❑   **dictionary**

Definition ....

Sentence ....

❑   **vocabulary**

Definition ....

Sentence ....

❑   **list(s)**

Definition ....

Sentence ....

❑   **need**

Definition ....

Sentence ....

❑   **expand**

Definition ....

Sentence ....

❑   **peer(s)**

Definition ....

Sentence ....

❑   **towel(s)**

Definition ....

Sentence ....

❑   **buckle(s)**

Definition ....

Sentence ....

❑   **high heel(s)**

Definition ....

Sentence ....

❑   **add**

Definition ....

Sentence ....

❑   **sportswear**

Definition ....

Sentence ....

❑   **aisle(s)**

Definition ....

Sentence ....

❑ **rack(s)**

Definition ....

Sentence ....

❑ **sweater(s)**

Definition ....

Sentence ....

❑ **politely**

Definition ....

Sentence ....

❑ **fit**

Definition ....

Sentence ....

❑ **hanger**

Definition ....

Sentence ....

❑ **almost**

Definition ....

Sentence ....

❑ **tax**

Definition ....

Sentence ....

❑ **comes to.....**

Definition ....

Sentence ....

❑ **I.D. or ID**

Definition ....

Sentence ....

❑ **research**

Definition ....

Sentence ....

❑ **compile**

Definition ....

Sentence ....

❑ **clerk(s)**

Definition ....

Sentence ....

❑ **discount**

Definition ....

Sentence ....

❑ **price(s)**
Definition ....
Sentence..
❑ **explanation(s)**
Definition ....
Sentence..
❑ **item(s)**
Definition ....
Sentence..
❑ **bar**
Definition ....
Sentence..
❑ **spending**
Definition ....
Sentence..
❑ **interesting**
Definition ....
Sentence..
❑ **reach**
Definition ....
Sentence..
❑ **limit(s)**
Definition ....
Sentence..

Exercise #2:-Learn the new words and look at the pictures of different clothes. Write the word and make a sentence with that word. For

example: **shirt**—I have a new blue shirt.

_____ --

221

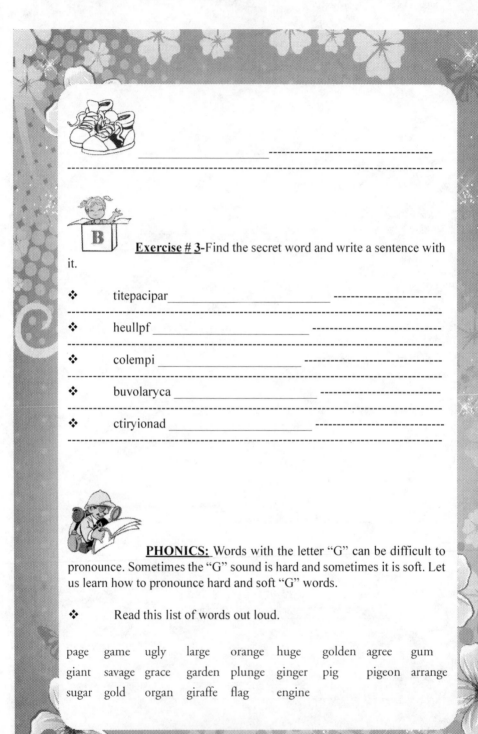

_____ -------------------------------------

Exercise # 3-Find the secret word and write a sentence with it.

❖　　titepacipar_____ ------------------------

❖　　heullpf_____ ----------------------------

❖　　colempi _____ ----------------------------

❖　　buvolaryca _____ ----------------------------

❖　　ctiryionad _____ ----------------------------

PHONICS: Words with the letter "G" can be difficult to pronounce. Sometimes the "G" sound is hard and sometimes it is soft. Let us learn how to pronounce hard and soft "G" words.

❖　　Read this list of words out loud.

page	game	ugly	large	orange	huge	golden	agree	gum
giant	savage	grace	garden	plunge	ginger	pig	pigeon	arrange
sugar	gold	organ	giraffe	flag	engine			

❖ Divide the words from the list into two groups. Under the **<u>flag</u>** write the words that contain a hard "G", under the **<u>orange</u>** write the words that contain a soft "G".

When "G" is followed by "e", "i", or "y", the "G" is usually soft. Soft "G" sounds like the sound "J".

When "G" is followed by "a", "o" or "u", the "G" sound is usually hard. Hard "G" sounds like the sound "G".

<u>Soft "G"</u>

<u>Hard "G"</u>

_____   _____

_____   _____

_____   _____

_____   _____

_____   _____

_____   _____

_____   _____

_____   _____

_____   _____

_____   _____

_____   _____

Phonics Exercise—Look and remember lists of **"G"** words when they are pronounced with a hard **"G"**.

O	A	U
GONE	GATE	GUM
GOAT	GAVE	GULL
GO	GAP	GUY
GOAL	GAZE	GUN
GOT	GARDEN	GUT
GOOSE	GAG	GULP
GOLD	GANG	GUARD
GOBLET	GOL	GUESS
GOES	GAS	GUEST
GOLD	GAY	GUIDE
GOLF	GAGE	GUT
GOOF	GAIN	GUMMY
GOOD	GARY	GUSHY
GOWN	GASP	GUST
GOFER	KANGAROO	FIGURE
GONE	MORGAN	REGULAR

Phonics Exercise—Colour only the cats that follow the rule for the soft **"G"** sound. If the letter **"G"** is in front of **"e"**, **"i"** or **"y"**, it usually takes the sound of the letter **"j"**. In this case it is called a soft **"G"**.

gem   gym   goat

gun   page   germ

giant   go   gate

go   magic   age

Phonics Exercise—Let us practice the rules. Read directions inside the picture.

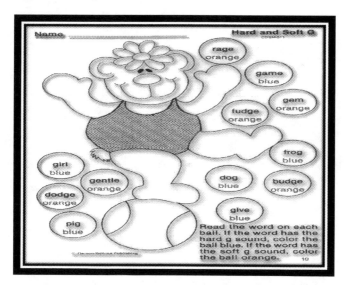

Name _____   Hard and Soft G

rage orange
game blue
gem orange
fudge orange
frog blue
girl blue
gentle orange
dog blue
budge orange
dodge orange
give blue
pig blue

Read the word on each ball. If the word has the hard g sound, color the ball blue. If the word has the soft g sound, color the ball orange.

Homework: Remember the rules and put the words in the list into three columns: Hard "G"; Soft "G" and both Hard and Soft "G".

gauge, general, giant, gymnastic, large, energy, geography, intelligible, changing, golf, pig, gorgeous, running, great, gum, fragrant, grasp, glut, progress, gigantic,

Hard "G"	Soft "G"	(Both) Hard and Soft "G"

STUDY TIP-If you learn the English pronunciation rules, you will be able to say the words correctly. It is essential to know all the pronunciation rules and apply them correctly when you read, write or speak.

SPOT THE MISTAKE-This dictionary helps people learn the correct information about a department store.........
....
....
....

....
....

REMEMBER THIS-Persistence is essential to success.

DID YOU KNOW? Banff National Park, located in the Province of Alberta, Canada is the oldest national park in Canada, established in 1885.

LANGUAGE BANK—In this lesson you learned:

Active words	Recycled words	Passive words
1. interested	1. ornament(s)	1. objective(s)
2. department store	2. totally	2. be able to . . . .
3. hate	3. enjoy	3. request
4. develop	4. stressful	4. information
5. exactly	5. disrupted	5. without
6. situation(s)	6. usually	6. presistence
7. participate	7. relationship(s)	7. enable

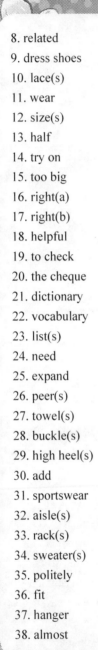

8. related
9. dress shoes
10. lace(s)
11. wear
12. size(s)
13. half
14. try on
15. too big
16. right(a)
17. right(b)
18. helpful
19. to check
20. the cheque
21. dictionary
22. vocabulary
23. list(s)
24. need
25. expand
26. peer(s)
27. towel(s)
28. buckle(s)
29. high heel(s)
30. add
31. sportswear
32. aisle(s)
33. rack(s)
34. sweater(s)
35. politely
36. fit
37. hanger
38. almost

8. agree
9. today
10. different
11. main
12. character
13. kind(s)
14. share
15. word(s)
16. expression(s)
17. improve
18. proficiency

Expressions: go shopping, window shop driver`s license, are going to . . . . excuse me, over there, how about . . . . how much, on sale, go ahead, in order to, fitting room, maxed out, make proud

8. context(s)
9. essential
10. apply
11. located
12. established
13. national
14. construct
15. general
16. giant(s)
17. energy
18. gymnastic
19. large
20. intelligible
21. golf
22. gum
23. fragrant
24. grasp(s)
25. glut
26. gauge(s)
27. geography
28. gigantic
29. gorgeous
30. fudge(s)
31. judge(s)
32. gem(s)
33. germ(s)
34. rage
35. range
36. gentle
37. lounge(s)
38. gin

39. tax

40. comes to . . . .

41. I.D. or ID

42. research

43. compile

44. clerk(s)

45. discount

46. price(s)

47. explanation(s)

48. item(s)

49. bar

50. spending

51. interesting

52. reach

53. limit(s)

39. magic

40. groan

41. lodg(s)e

42. globe(s)

43. merge

44. tiger(s)

Check Your Knowledge

Let us review our knowledge

Task #1-Review the vocabulary you learned in this book.

 Lesson 1—English Alphabet

LANGUAGE BANK—In this lesson you learned:

Active words	Recycled words	Passive words
1. letter(s)	1. day(s)	1. country
2. the sound(s)	2. class(es)	2. world(s)
3. alphabet	3. student(s)	3. about
4. know	4. come	4. anybody
5. say	5. learn	5. achieve
6. name(s)	6. some	6. goal(s)
7. remember	7. word(s)	7. need
8. question(s)	8. but	8. wait
9. hard	9. new	9. enter
10. different	10. thing(s)	10. greet
11. problem(s)	11. read	11. shy
12. spelling	12. this	12. embarrassed
13. properly	13. sit	13. excited
14. to check	14. classroom(s)	14. voice(s)
15. tool(s)	15. teacher(s)	15. agree
16. correct	16. computer(s)	16. using
17. everyone	17. sentence(s)	17. everything
18. certain	18. sometimes	
19. exist	19. because	

20. recognize
21. right
22. (to) sound
23. spell
24. mark
25. something
26. mistake(s)
27. champion(s)
28. province
29. mean
30. explain
31. express
32. agreement(s)
33. idea(s)
34. (to) hand
35. important
36. depend
37. want
38. think
39. look
40. the same
41. need
42. true
43. understand

20. help
21. strong
22. tomorrow

Expressions: by heart, don't worry, proof reading, right place, rules of pronunciation, I am ready, importance of learning, test your knowledge

Lesson 2—Beginning Consonants

LANGUAGE BANK—In this lesson you learned:

Active words	Recycled words	Passive words
1. consonant(s)	1. word(s)	1. today
2. beginning	2. new	2. second
3. yesterday	3. learn	3. bear(s)
4. afternoon	4. day(s)	4. bee(s)
5. went-go	5. help	5. beaver(s)
6. we	6. say	6. bat(s)
7. vocabulary	7. different	7. butterfly
8. too	8. nice	8. cow(s)
9. are speaking	9. spring	9. chick(s)
10. clear	10. warm	10. camel(s)
11. voice(s)	11. many	11. crocodile(s)

12. paper(s)
13. collect
14. improve
15. exercise(s)
16. enjoy-ed
17. easy
18. vowel(s)
19. there are
20. practise
21. express

12. flower(s)
13. learn-ed
14. was hard
15. to hand in
16. spell
17. problem(s)
18. question(s)

12. chameleon(s)
13. crab(s)
14. donkey
15. duck(s)
16. deer
17. dove(s)
18. dolphin(s)
19. fawn
20. fish
21. frog(s)
22. fox(es)
23. fly
24. flamingo(s)
25. giraffe
26. goose
27. goat(s)
28. grasshopper(s)
29. hen(s)
30. horse(s)
31. jelly fish
32. jackal
33. jaguar(s)
34. koala(s)
35. kangaroo
36. kitten(s)
37. lion(s)
38. leopard(s)
39. llama(s)
40. lamb(s)
41. ladybug(s)
42. mouse

Expressions: I am so proud of you, it is my pleasure, I am able, make mistakes, all of you, pay attention to . . . . , practice makes perfect

43. monkey(s)
44. mosquito(es)
45. newspaper(s)
46. pig(s)
47. piglet(s)
48. puppy
49. parrot(s)
50. penguin(s)
51. peacock(s)
52. question mark(s)
53. rabbit(s)
54. rooster(s)
55. spider(s)
56. seal(s)
57. swan(s)
58. sheep(s)
59. snail(s)
60. snake(s)
61. turtle(s)
62. turkey
63. vine(s)
64. Valentine
65. whale(s)
66. wolf
67. yoyo(s)
68. yarn

Cc Lesson 3—Short" a", "o" and "æ"

LANGUAGE BANK—In this lesson you learned:

Active words	**Recycled words**	**Passive words**
1. late	1. it is	1. start(ed)
2. told/tell	2. nice	2. turn
3. come	3. yellow	3. for example
4. concerned	4. student(s)	4. apologize
5. what	5. today	5. finish
6. sick	6. classroom(s)	6. to end
7. think	7. school(s)	7. verse
8. play(ed)	8. improve	8. print
9. ice	9. voice(s)	9. each
10. water	10. easy	10. pair(s)
11. throat(s)	11. speak	11. use
12. why	12. yesterday	12. rhyme(s)
13. how	13. afternoon	13. ham

14. can
15. phone
16. give
17. idea (s)
18. wonderful
19. the same
20. apple(s)
21. hope
22. us
23. inetrnational
24. system(s)
25. symbol(s)
26. correct
27. pronounce
28. pronunciation
29. must
30. even
31. let us

14. went
15. home(s)
16. paper(s)
17. because
18. clear
19. flower(s)
20. cherries
21. strawberries
22. too
23. exercise(s)
24. practice
25. collect
26. everybody
27. agree
28. need
29. ask
30. question(s)
31. excited
32. mean

33. sound(s)
34. expression(s)

14. bank(s)
15. number(s)
16. dad(s)
17. cap(s)
18. bag(s)
19. map(s)
20. bad
21. top(s)
22. stop
23. not
24. doll(s)
25. frog(s)
26. good

Expressions: I am so sorry, no worries

it is fine, have a sore throat,

I am sure, take good notes,

are/am/ going to . . . .

Lesson 4—My New Country
Ending Sounds

LANGUAGE BANK—In this lesson you learned:

Active words	**Recycled words**	**Passive words**
1. some	1. come	1. recently
2. province(s)	2. they	2. originally
3. territory	3. want	3. important
4. yesterday	4. learn	4. exercise(s)
5. question(s)	5. new	5. mistake(s)
6. that	6. country	6. language(s)
7. focus	7. lesson	7. bank(s)
8. understand	8. clasroom	8. remember
9. same	9. today	10. enter
10. research	10. anybody	11. any
11. problem (s)	11. go	12. more
12. did/do	12. answer(s)	13. noun(s)

13. decision(s)
14. federal
15. government(s)
16. newspaper
17. divide(d)
18. part(s)
19. area(s)
20. call(ed)
21. large(est)
22. equal
23. capital(s)
24. population
25. above
26. dogsled(s)
27. snowmobile(s)
28. to fish
29. to hunt
30. seal(s)
31. meat
32. boot(s)
33. skin
34. fat
35. help(ed)
36. /think/thought
37. change(d)
38. right
39. vocabulary
40. find/found
41. magazine(s)
42. month(s)
43. frozen

13. thank you
14. spring
15. winter
16. animal
18. people
19. what

14. common
15. proper
16. name(s)
17. frienship
18. happiness

44. which
45. different
46. their
47. improve(d)
48. use(d)
49. airplane(s)
50. food(s)
51. difference
52. between
53. constitutional
54. power(s)
55. govern(ed)

Expressions: of course, I am not sure, made up of, in the old days, on the other hand, move around, lamp oil

Lesson # 5—Facts about Canada
"TH" Sound

LANGUAGE BANK—In this lesson you learned:

Active words	Recycled words	Passive words
1. discussion(s)	1. province	1. project
2. collect	2. territory	2. slide(s)
3. important	3. research	3. screen(s)
4. to present	4. start	4. plural
5. library	5. fact	5. form
6. easy	6. their	6. singular
7. to show	7. questions	7. vowel(s)
8. drawing(s)	8. homework	8. consider
9. glad	9. today	9. notebook(s)
10. choose	10. focus	10. powerpoint
11. idea(s)	11. everyone	11. presentation

12. smart
13. althought
14. inhabit
15. way(s)
16. interesting
17. survival
18. skill(s)
19. walrus
20. feed
21. protect
22. add
23. prepare
24. something
25. listen
26. leave
27. deep
28. sea
29. cry
30. are born
31. also
32. month(s)
33. cub(s)

12. was sure
13. found
14. different
15. some
16. animal(s)
17. area
18. is made up of
19. warm
20. want
21. anybody
22. of course

12. make sure
13. cover slide
14. at least

Expressions: all kinds of, take care of, at first

Lesson 6—Words from Immigrants
Confusing Letters

LANGUAGE BANK—In this lesson you learned:

Active words	**Recycled words**	**Passive words**
1. immigrant(s)	1. learn	1. usually
2. main	2. sound(s)	2. need
3. topic(s)	3. both	3. secret(s)
4. bring(brought)	4. word(s)	4. violin(s)
5. contribution(s)	5. glad	5. hump(s)
6. special	6. some	6. ice cream
7. confusing	7. know	7. jelly
8. good(better)	8. different	8. prince(s)
9. employment	9. language(s)	9. queen(s)
10. become	10. discussion(s)	10. circle(s)
11. responsibility	11. focus	11. belong
12. sometimes	12. problem(s)	12. shape(s)

13. enrich
14. example(s)
15. history
16. easy
17. ham
18. think
19. true
20. connected
21. seaport(s)
22. share
23. European(s)
24. line(s)
25. food
26. ate(eat)
27. patty
28. grill
29. serve
30. bun(s)
31. understand
32. exist
33. to form
34. popular
35. fast
36. which
37. confuse
38. pronounce

13. important
14. of course
15. population
16. leave
17. part(s)
18. way(s)
19. town(s)
20. travel
21. right

13. culture(s)
14. purpose(s)
15. arrive

Expressions: getting older, on the other hand, make appoint, made out of, in fact, at that time, ground beef.

Lesson 7—Animal World
Short and Long vowel "u"

LANGUAGE BANK—In this lesson you learned:

Active words	**Recycled words**	**Passive words**
1. insect(s)	1. discussion	1. dictionary
2. science	2. focus	2. check
3. weather	3. animal(s)	3. following
4. go-went	4. interesting	4. copy
5. shelter(s)	5. smart	5. description
6. pet	6. understand	6. secret(s)
7. until	7. special	7. hug(s)
8. adopt	8. which	8. mug(s)
9. milk	9. form	9. bug(s)
10. drink	10. cow(s)	10. truck(s)
11. goat(s)	11. like	11. definition(s)

12. always
13. dirty
14. mud
15. must
16. never
17. lamb(s)
18. breakfast
19. sometimes
20. duck(s)
21. hen(s)

22. rooster(s)
23. share
24. duckling(s)
25. year(s)
26. family
27. bee(s)
28. butterfly
29. ladybug(s)
30. worm(s)
31. honey
32. antenna(s)
33. wing(s)
34. pretty
35. woods
36. mosquito(s)
37. female(s)
38. bite
39. protein
40. produce
41. male

12. too
13. anybody
14. little
15. summer
16. think
17. anything
18. know
19. read
20. right
21. drink

22. because
23. excercise(s)
24. warm
25. a lot of
26. beautiful
27. grass
28. eat
29. field(s)
30. class(es)
31. word(s)
32. discuss
33. about
34. story
35. play
36. smell
37. confused
38. something

12. nearly
13. mean
14. express
15. different
16. period
17. synonym(s)

Expressions: pick out, fresh food,

trip, take a break, camping

42. feed on
43. prevent
43. perfume
44. ruin

Lesson 8—Celebrations
Short vowel "i"

LANGUAGE BANK—In this lesson you learned:

Active words	Recycled words	Passive words
1. holiday(s)	1. question(s)	1. folks
2. celebration(s)	2. main	2. change
3. celebrate	3. fall	3. movies
4. glorious	4. day(s)	4. sounds
5. notice	5. tree(s)	5. internally
6. marvelous	6. season(s)	6. externally
7. October	7. beautiful	7. divide
8. television	8. special	8. establish
9. typical	9. people	9. incorporate
10. scary	10. right	10. mind
11. neighbourhood	11. blood	11. correlate

12. character(s)
13. ghost(s)
14. silly
15. poor
16. experience
17. promise(s)
18. the dead
19. pray
20. treat(s)
21. candy
22. thankful
23. decorate
24. ornament(s)
25. need
26. under
27. tie
28. bow
29. come
30. present(s)
31. ready
32. stocking(s)
33. popular
34. lovely
35. turned
36. delicious

12. eye(s)
13. talk about
14. sound
15. think
16. go/went
17. house
18. popular
19. library
20. children
21. help
22. connect
23. a lot of
24. different
25. the same
26. sometimes
27. share
28. wavy lines
29. some
30. painted
31. lemon cake
32. about

12. previously

Expressions—All Souls Day, trick-and-treat, drop out, in front of. jack-o-lantern, make sure, wake up

Jj

Jaguar

Lesson # 9—Travelling
Short vowel "e"

LANGUAGE BANK—In this lesson you learned:

Active words	Recycled words	Passive words
1. travelling	1. student	1. topic
2. trip(s)	2. come	2. however
3. difficult	3. country	3. but
4. driving	4. leave-left	4. when
5. storm(s)	5. old	5. after
6. road(s)	6. experience(s)	6. definition(s)
7. slippery	7. share	7. pair(s)
8. usually	8. must	8. sound
9. bus	9. morning	9. each other
10. train(s)	10. winter	10. confused
11. drive-drop	11. night	11. easily

12. appointment(s)

13. ride

14. bicycle(s)

15. plane(s)

16. nervous

17. during

18. vacation(s)

19. place(s)

20. last

21. visit

22. ferry

23. take/took

24. faster

25. truck(s)

26. passing

27. conductor

28. homophones(s)

29. synonym(s)

30. antonym(s)

31. meaning(s)

32. explain

33. alike

34. spelling

35. another

36. almost

37. need

38. opposite

39. concept(s)

40. practice

41. totally

12. car

13. cold

14. like

15. summer

16. different

17. go-went

18. live

19. grandmother

20. too

21. house

22. important

23. something

Expressions: have the chance, I am sorry, come across, make a point

12. be careful

13. correct

14 express something

15. meaning

16. entrance

17. envelope

18. elephant

19. first time

20. really

21. forest/woods

22. shut/close

23. tale/story

24. hurt/injure

25. quiet/still

26. protect/guard

27. wet/dry

28. light/dark

29. light/heavy

30. strong/weak

31. loose/tight

32. lose/win

33. spend/save

34. sharp/dull

35. fearless/fearful

36. fat/thin

37. bright/dull

38. friend/enemy

39. asleep/awake

40. full/empty

41. hard/soft

42. agree

43. exercise(s)

42. quiet/noisy

43. over/under

44. climb/descend

Lesson 10—My Body, My Health
Short a + r

LANGUAGE BANK—In this lesson you learned:

Active words	Recycled words	Passive words
1. proficiency	1. happy	1. between
2. especially	2. student(s)	2. only
3. pronunciation	3. know	3. using
4. spelling	4. remember	4. when
5. communicate	5. expression(s)	5. just
6. connect	6. word(s)	6. through
7. health	7. today	7. healthy
8. medicine	8. body	8. true
9. cardiologist	9. home(s)	9. always
10. accident(s)	10. come	
11. become	11. drive	

12. patient(s)
13. toe(s)
14. itchy
15. peely
16. blister(s)
17. sign(s)
18. treated
19. cracked
20. skin
21. important
22. scratch
23. spread
24. share
25. smoking
26. bad
27. habit(s)
28. drug(s)
29. decision(s)
30. mind
31. tobacco
32. contain
33. substance(s)
34. addictive
35. cigarette(s)
36. cigar(s)
37. poison(s)
38. mouth(s)
39. throat(s)
40. lung(s)

12. trip(s)
13. road(s)
14. slippery
15. doctor(s)
16. dry
17. usually
18. situation(s)
19. sound(s)
20. difficult
21. easily
22. show
23. drawing
24. something
25. called
26. smell

Expressions: work hard, right now, grow up, pay attention,

no matter, peer pressure, make healthy choices, heart

attack, all at once, keep in mind

41. pollute

42. breath

43. affect

44. appearance(s)

45. exposure(s)

46. fingernail(s)

47. accept

48. million(s)

49. world

50. unique

51. magazine(s)

52. fabulous

53. inside

54. age

55. attractive

56. brace(s)

Lesson 11—Emotional Health
Hard and Soft "C"

LANGUAGE BANK—In this lesson you learned:

Active words	Recycled words	Passive words
1. believe	1. discussion(s)	1. highway
2. feeling(s)	2. healthy	2. keep writing
3. continue	3. choice(s)	3. world
4. same	4. yesterday	4. national
5. topic(s)	5. today	5. length
6. behaviour	6. think	6, mile(s)
7. stress	7. important	7. idea(s)
8. relationship(s)	8. comment(s)	8. building
9. happen	9. situation(s)	9. vocabulary
10. disrupt	10. child	10. learning
11. sadness	11. sick	11. context
12. anxiety	12. medicine	12. material

13. main
14. characteristic(s)
15. deal with
16. death
17. move to
18. change(s)
19. stressful
20. affect
21. respond
22. connection(s)
23. upset
24. disease(s)
25. develop
26. pain(s)
27. appetite
28. headache
29. gain
30. weight
31. lose
32. exercising
33. alcohol
34. recognize
35. cause(s)
36. inside
37. outside
38. bothering
39. counselor(s)
40. balanced
41. journal(s)
42. sleep

13. especially
14. sound
15. strong
16. tobacco
17. drug(s)
18. take care of
19. take
20. find
21. share
22. someone
23. happy
24. focus
25. improve
26. number
27. research

13. effective
14. certain
15. try
16. systematic
17. spoken
18. hard
19. soft
20. strip
21. decide
22. cut
23. paste

Expressions: emotional health, be aware of, cope with stress, be interested in . . ., lose the job, lose weight, get married, get divorced, high blood pressure, keep in mind, make time for . . . .

43. resilience
44. social
45. support
46. accept
47. calm
48. relaxation
49. meditation
50. regular

Mm

Lesson 12—Shopping for clothes
Hard and Soft "G"

LANGUAGE BANK—In this lesson you learned:

Active words	Recycled words	Passive words
1. interested	1. ornament(s)	1. objective(s)
2. department store	2. totally	2. be able to . . . .
3. hate	3. enjoy	3. request
4. develop	4. stressful	4. information
5. exactly	5. disrupted	5. without
6. situation(s)	6. usually	6. presistence
7. participate	7. relationship(s)	7. enable
8. related	8. agree	8. context(s)
9. dress shoes	9. today	9. essential
10. lace(s)	10. different	10. apply

11. wear
12. size(s)
13. half
14. try on
15. too big
16. right(a)
17. right(b)
18. helpful
19. to check
20. the cheque
21. dictionary
22. vocabulary
23. list(s)
24. need
25. expand
26. peer(s)
27. towel(s)
28. buckle(s)
29. high heel(s)
30. add
31. sportswear
32. aisle(s)
33. rack(s)
34. sweater(s)
35. politely
36. fit
37. hanger
38. almost

11. main
12. character
13. kind(s)
14. share
15. word(s)
16. expression(s)
17. improve
18. proficiency

Expressions: go shopping, window shop

driver`s license, are going to . . . .

excuse me, over there, how about . . . .

how much, on sale, go ahead,

in order to, fitting room, maxed out,

make proud

11. located
12. established
13. national
14. construct
15. general
16. giant(s)
17. energy
18. gymnastic
19. large
20. intelligible
21. golf
22. gum
23. fragrant
24. grasp(s)
25. glut
26. gauge(s)
27. geography
28. gigantic
29. gorgeous
30. fudge(s)
31. judge(s)
32. gem(s)
33. germ(s)
34. rage
35. range
36. gentle
37. lounge(s)
38. gin

39. tax

40. comes to . . . .

41. I.D. or ID

42. research

43. compile

44. clerk(s)

45. discount

46. price(s)

47. explanation(s)

48. item(s)

49. bar

50. spending

51. interesting

52. reach

53. limit(

39. magic

40. groan

41. lodg(s)e

42. globe(s)

43. merge

44. tiger(s)

Task # 2—Vocabulary Review—Pair work: Review the new words with a friend. Take turns saying the word and asking for a definition and a sentence.

Student # 1—Please, give definitions and sentences for these words:

❖ **shelter**

Definition ....

Sentence ....

❖ **dirty**

Definition ....

Sentence ....

❖ **breakfast**

Definition ....

Sentence ....

❖ **butterfly**

Definition ....

Sentence ....

❖ **honey**

Definition ....

Sentence ....

❖ **wear**

Definition ....

Sentence ....

❖ **laces**

Definition ....

Sentence ....

❖ **to check**

Definition ....

Sentence ....

❖ **the cheque**

Definition ....

Sentence ....

❖ **expand**

Definition ....

Sentence ....

❖ **vocabulary**

Definition ....

Sentence ....

❖ **peer**

Definition ....

Sentence ....

❖ **add**

Definition ....

Sentence ....

❖ **sweater**

Definition ....

Sentence ....

❖ **aisle**

Definition ....

Sentence ....

❖ **discount**

Definition ....

Sentence...

❖ **explanation**

Definition ....

Sentence...

❖ **limit**

Definition ....

Sentence...

Student #2—Please, give definitions and sentences for the following words:

❖ **stocking**

Definition ....

Sentence...

❖ **present**

Definition ....

Sentence...

❖ **party**

Definition ....

Sentence...

❖ **trip**

Definition ....

Sentence...

❖ **difficult**

Definition ....

Sentence...

❖ **appointment**

Definition ....

Sentence...

❖ **bicycle**

Definition ....

Sentence...

❖ **nervous**

Definition ....

Sentence...

❖   **vacation**

Definition ....

Sentence ....

❖   **homophone**

Definition ....

Sentence ....

❖   **protect**

Definition ....

Sentence ....

❖   **antonym**

Definition ....

Sentence ....

❖   **proficiency**

Definition ....

Sentence ....

❖   **connect**

Definition ....

Sentence ....

Task # 3-Review correct pronunciation of vowels:

a) Draw a circle around the vowel and say the word out loud. Remember the rules of pronunciation you have learned in this book. There is a list of the main rules for quick reference on the inside cover of this book.

A	I	U	O	E
can	kite	cute	hop	eat
came	kit	bun	home	peg
had	rip	tub	hot	red
late	ride	muff	bone	desk
man	milk	cube	lost	peak
rain	pick	nuts	got	neck

fat	tin	flute	pop	feel
mail	time	fun	note	web
gas	lick	fuse	fog	let
jam	wide	tune	tone	seem
tame	fin	tub	Tom	bed
lap	pipe	hum	dog	reap
an	pill	rule	rock	tent
cab	hid	cub	cone	peel
wax	fix	tube	goat	jet
name	pine	up	block	went
tail	miss	use	rode	she
Sam	hide	rub	road	Ben
ask	is	dust	lock	belt
ate	big	pure	top	deep
last	dime	hut	job	pen
sand	lift	us	no	elf
pain	hill	bug	box	men
Ann	bike	Luke	toss	leap

Task # 4—Find the secret word and write a sentence with it.

❖ titepacipar_____ -----------------------------

❖ heullpf_____ -----------------------------

❖ alrexniaot_____ -----------------------------

❖ ecreienlis_____ -----------------------------

- ❖ ecnyicifpro_____ -------------------------------------

- ❖ diooltsigdrac_____ -------------------------------------

- ❖ ainrt_____ ---

- ❖ yrref_____ ---

- ❖ unat_____ ---

- ❖ ouslevram_____ ---

- ❖ sluogiour_____ --

- ❖ yfltertbu_____ ---------------------------------------

- ❖ ucedopro_____ --

- ❖ entmyoemlp_____ ------------------------------------

- ❖ ilytbiisrenops_____ ----------------------------------

- ❖ nttaoripm—_____ ---------------------------------------

- ❖ uhgohtla-_____ ---

Task # 5—Write the letter that comes after each of these consonants in the English alphabet in the following list.

m____   q____   n____   p____   g____   r____   v____

x____   z____   c____   s____   d____   f____   w____

h___   b___   j___   k___   l___   t____   y____

Task # 6—Write the letter that comes after each vowel of the alphabet in the following list:

o____   a____   i____   e____   u____

Task # 7—Copy, colour and cut out the fish. Look at the letters under each fish and paste the letter on the correct Fish Tank.

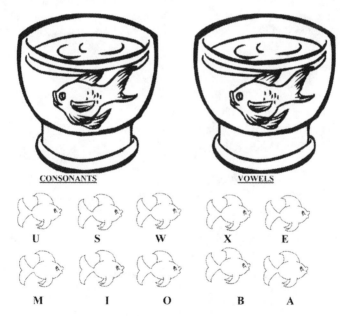

CONSONANTS   VOWELS

U   S   W   X   E

M   I   O   B   A

Task # 8-Let us learn some antonyms, check their meaning in your dictionary. Write the correct word from Column II beside its antonym in Column I.

I	II	I	II	I	II
strong _____	light	light _____	tight	large _____	fearful
dry _____	few	loose _____	warm	sharp _____	spend
hot _____	wet	cold _____	dull	sick _____	dull
dark _____	weak	fat _____	heavy	fearless _____	healthy
many _____	cold	bright _____	thin	save _____	small

Task # 9—Let us practice using the correct homophones. Draw a circle around the word that correctly completes each sentence. Then write the complete sentence on the line provided. Look at the example: We asked the (maid, made) to wash the windows. <u>We asked the maid to wash the windows.</u>

❑ The wind (blew, blue) the clouds away. _____

❑ Eric (cent, sent) his puzzle to a friend. _____

❑ We are learning to (right, write) English. _____

❑ Mother was very (weak, week) after being sick. _____

❑ Cindy (through, threw) the ball and broke the window. _____

❑ We (ate, eight) our supper early. _____

❑ The doctor will (be, bee) here in a minute. _____

❑ He went to the shop to (by, buy) a new software. _____

Task # 10—Remember the rules and put the words from the follwoing list into three columns: Hard "G"; Soft "G" and both Hard and Soft "G".

gauge, general, giant, gymnastic, large, energy, geography, intelligible, changing, golf, pig, gorgeous, running, great, gum, fragrant, grasp, glut, progress, gigantic,

Hard "G"	Soft "G"	(Both) Hard and Soft "G"

Task # 11—Winnie the Walrus is picky about the fish she eats. She likes only fish that start with the same beginning sound as—wet-. Circle the words under the fish that Winnie the Walrus likes to eat.

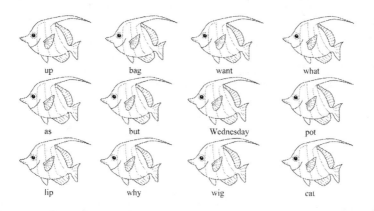

up   bag   want   what

as   but   Wednesday   pot

lip   why   wig   cat

Progress Exam

Exercise #1—Write the definition and a sentence with the word in bold.

1.　　**communicate**
Definition ....
Sentence ....
2.　　**cardiologist**
Definition ....
Sentence ....
3.　　**patient**
Definition ....
Sentence ....
4.　　**blister**
Definition ....
Sentence ....
5.　　**important**
Definition ....
Sentence ....
6.　　**habit**
Definition ....
Sentence ....
7.　　**mouth**
Definition ....
Sentence ....
8.　　**pollute**
Definition ....
Sentence ....
9.　　**fabulous**
Definition ....
Sentence ....

10. **attractive**
Definition ....
Sentence...
11. **feeling**
Definition ....
Sentence...
12. **believe**
Definition ....
Sentence...
13. **topic**
Definition ....
Sentence...
14. **behavior**
Definition ....
Sentence...
15. **characteristic**
Definition ....
Sentence...

Score _____/15

Exercise #2—Finish each rhyme with a word that rhymes with the first word.

a bed with a _ _ _ _

a pet that is _ _ _

a bell and a _ _ _ _

a pet in a _ _ _

Score _____/4

Exercise #2—Find the mistakes and write the correct word next to each picture.

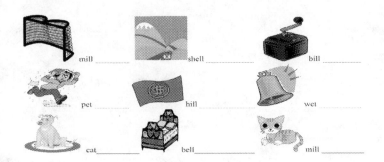

mill _____   shell _____   bill _____

pet _____   hill _____   wet _____

cat _____   bell _____   mill _____

Score _____ /8

Exercise # 3—Colour the candy red if it has a vowel under it. Colour the candy blue if it has a consonant under it.

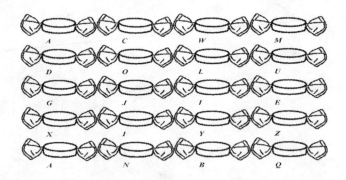

Score _____ /20

Exercise # 4—Find the short "i" words **bib, fish, hill, fin, lid, pin**. Circle, and color them in yellow. The words in the table go ➜➜(horizontally) and ⬇ (vertically).
⬇

F	M	B	I	B	K	G
I	W	U	T	L	I	D
N	R	I	P	V	J	E
C	A	X	F	I	S	H
X	H	I	L	L	Q	M
P	I	N	Z	Y	O	Z

Score _____/12

Exercise # 5—Read and write these words. Pay special attention to "the" sound. Is the sound a [θ]sound or a [ð]sound? Write the pronunciation of each word in IPA alphabet.

bath [ ],   with [ ],   month [ ],   these [ ],   path [ ],   this [ ]

math [ ],   thin [ ],   then [ ],   them [ ],   thing [ ],   thank[ ]

there [ ],   thick[ ],   they [ ],   than [ ],   those [ ],   math [ ]

this [ ],   that [ ]

Score _____/10

Exercise # 6-Look at the words: if the word has a soft G-sound, colour brown; if the word has a hard G-sound, colour yellow.

Name_____

Hard and Soft G

CDSM-511

germ
brown

goat
yellow

flag
yellow

egg
yellow

range
brown

good
yellow

angel
brown

gave
yellow

lounge
brown

magic
brown

cage
brown

goose
yellow

fudge
brown

goes
yellow

gin
brown

forgot
yellow

Read the word on each kernel of carmel corn. If the word has a hard g sound, color the kernel yellow. If the word has a soft g sound, color the kernel brown.

12

Score _____/10

274

Exercise # 7—Circle the words that start with the same sound

as the word "whale"  . Then find and colour in yellow the words in the puzzle. Here is the list: whack, watch, whip, which, wish.

R	W	W	H	A	C	K	B
K	H	N	W	A	T	C	H
C	I	W	I	S	H	I	T
G	C	H	C	I	H	S	Y
W	H	I	P	X	E	I	Z
Q	H	Z	I	U	N	W	M
W	H	I	C	H	I	H	N
Z	S	R	N	K	W	E	W

Score _____ **/21**

Total Score _____ **/100**

Correct mistakes.

Here are your mistakes, write each word at home again:

CONGRATULATIONS!

END OF BOOK # 4

(You can proceed to book #2 if your test score is 85% or more)

Guide to Pronunciation Symbols

Vowels

Symbol	Key Word	Pronunciation
/ɑ/	Hot	/hɑt/
	Far	/fɑr/
/æ/	Cat	/kæt/
/aɪ/	fine	/faɪn/
/aʊ/	house	/haʊs/
/ɛ/	bed	/bɛd/
/eɪ/	name	/neɪm/
/i/	need	/nid/
/ɪ/	sit	/sɪt/
/oʊ/	go	/goʊ/
/ʊ/	book	/bʊk/
/ɔ/	dog	/dɔg/
	four	/fɔr/
/ɔɪ/	toy	/tɔɪ/
/ʌ/	cup	/kʌp/
/ɚr/	bird	/bɝd/
/ə/	about	/əˈbaʊt/
	after	/ˈæftər/

Consonants

Symbol	Key Word	Pronunciation
/b/	boy	/bɔɪ/
/d/	day	/deɪ/
/dʒ/	just	/dʒʌst/
/f/	face	/feɪs/
/g/	get	/gɛt/
/h/	hat	/hæt/
/k/	car	/kɑr/
/l/	light	/laɪt/
/m/	my	/maɪ/
/n/	nine	/naɪn/
/ŋ/	sing	/sɪŋ/
/p/	pen	/pɛn/
/ɾ/	right	/ɾaɪt/
/s/	see	/si/
/t/	tea	/ti/
/ʧ/	cheap	/ʧip/
/v/	vote	/voʊt/
/w/	west	/wɛst/
/y/	yes	/yɛs/
/z/	zoo	/zu/
/ð/	they	/ðeɪ/

/θ/	think	/θɪŋk/
/ʃ/	shoe	/ʃu/
/ʒ/	vision	/ˈvɪʒən/

Appendix # 1

Pronunciation of Vowels in English

Following are the vowels used in Canadian English. The way the symbols have been used is very close to the way they should be used in the International Phonetical Alphabet (IPA).

i

machine	[mə'ʃin]
heed	[hid]
beat, beet	[bit]
sneak	[snik]

I "small or capital I"

bit	[bɪt]
miss	[mɪs]
hid	[hɪd]

e

passé	[pæ'se]
bait	[bet]
hayed	[hed]
make	[mek]
steak, stake	[stek]

ε the Greek letter "epsilon"—[ˈɛpsəlɑn]

head [hɛd]

bet [bɛt]

many [ˈmɛni]

æ "diagraph"

had [hæd]

bat [bæt]

ɑ "script-a"

father [fɑðəɹ]

bought [bɑt]

caught, cot [kɑt]

law [lɑ]

o

hoed [hod]

boat [bot]

low [lo]

beau [bo]

ʊ

put	[pʊt]
hood	[hʊd]
book	[bʊk]

u

blue	[blu]
who'd	[hud]
boot	[but]
drew	[dɹu]

ʌ "caret"

but	[bʌt]
cup	[kʌp]
double	[dʌbəl]

aj

I, eye	[aj]
fly	[flaj]
bite	[bajt]
hide	[hajd]
might	[majt]

aw

cow   [kaw]

bout   [bawt]

ɔj

toy   [tɔj]

Boyd   [bɔjd]

noise   [nɔjz]

ə "schwa"—the neutral vowel

banana   [bə'nænə]